Published by
Rupa Publications India Pvt. Ltd 2025
7/16, Ansari Road, Daryaganj
New Delhi 110002

Sales centres:
Bengaluru Chennai
Hyderabad Jaipur Kathmandu
Kolkata Mumbai Prayagraj

Copyright © Rupa Publications India Pvt. Ltd 2025

The views and opinions expressed in this book are the
authors' own and the facts are as reported by him which
have been verified to the extent possible, and the publishers
are not in any way liable for the same.

All rights reserved.
No part of this publication may be reproduced, transmitted,
or stored in a retrieval system, in any form or by any means,
electronic, mechanical, photocopying, recording or otherwise,
without the prior permission of the publisher.

Photo Source: Wikimedia Commons

ISBN: 978-93-6156-525-0

First impression 2025

10 9 8 7 6 5 4 3 2 1

The moral right of the author has been asserted.

Printed in India

This book is sold subject to the condition that it shall not,
by way of trade or otherwise, be lent, resold, hired out, or otherwise
circulated, without the publisher's prior consent, in any form of
binding or cover other than that in which it is published.

CONTENTS

Introduction		5
1.	The History of Golf: from Pastime to Professional Sport	9

SECTION ONE
GETTING STARTED

2.	Understanding Golf: The Art of the Game	24
3.	Essential Equipment and Gear for Golf Enthusiasts	46
4.	Golf Stance and Movement: Mastering the Foundation of the Game	53
5.	Basic Golf Techniques and Combinations: Mastering the Fundamentals	63
6.	Defensive Techniques in Golf: Mastering Control and Consistency	74
7.	Practice Grounds and Precision	84
8.	Mental Mastery on the Green	91

9.	Physical Conditioning for Golfers	99
10.	Fueling the Swing: Nutrition and Diet for Golfers	109
11.	Precision Mastery: Elevating Your Golfing Skills	114
12.	Embarking on Your First Golf Tournament: A Comprehensive Guide	122
13.	Refining Your Strategy: Analyzing Competitions for Golf	132
14.	The Future of Golf	143
15.	Nurturing the Next Olympic Golfer	150
16	Filipino Olympians in Golf Sports	154
List of Olympic Medalists In Golf (1900, 1904, 2016-2024)		159

INTRODUCTION

GOLF IS MORE THAN JUST STRIKING A BALL WITH A CLUB—it's a complex blend of precision, strategy, and mental endurance. Whether playing a casual round with friends or competing in high-stakes tournaments, golf demands a deep understanding of technique, course management, and the psychological aspects of the game. The sport challenges individuals to master not only their physical skills but also their ability to maintain composure under pressure. From the serene beauty of the golf course to the tension of sinking a critical putt, golf is a game that requires focus, patience, and an unwavering commitment to improvement.

This book is designed to guide you through the intricate world of golf, offering insights into its rich history, the evolution of equipment and techniques, and the mental and physical conditioning required to excel. At its core, golf is a test of precision and consistency. Each shot involves a careful orchestration of stance, grip, swing, and follow-through—every movement deliberate and purposeful.

Golf has grown into a global phenomenon, with events like The Masters and The Open Championship attracting players and spectators from around the world. The sport is as much about personal mastery as it is about competition, with each round offering new challenges and opportunities for growth.

THE EVOLUTION OF GOLF: FROM SHEPHERDS TO CHAMPIONS

From its humble beginnings with shepherds using rudimentary clubs to knock stones into rabbit holes on the rugged Scottish terrain, golf has transformed into a sport of precision, strategy, and global appeal. The early game, with its crude equipment and lack of formal rules, was more pastime than sport, but it laid the foundation for what would become one of the most challenging and revered sports in the world.

The formalization of golf began in the 18th century, with the establishment of the first golf clubs and the standardization of the game's rules. As the sport grew in popularity, the development of more sophisticated equipment, such as the introduction of the gutta-percha ball and iron-headed clubs, allowed for greater precision and control, revolutionizing the way the game was played.

The modern era of golf is defined by its diversity of disciplines, including stroke play, match play, and team competitions like the Ryder Cup. Each format brings its own unique challenges and strategies, and each has its own place in the rich tapestry of the sport's history.

Golf has produced legendary figures such as Jack Nicklaus, Arnold Palmer, and Tiger Woods, who have not only dominated the sport but have also helped to popularize it around the globe. These champions have set records, won countless tournaments, and inspired millions of players to take up the game.

As golf continues to evolve, innovations in technology and equipment, such as the use of GPS in course management and advanced materials in club manufacturing, are pushing the boundaries of what is possible on the course. The introduction of biomechanical analysis and data-driven training methods has also enhanced players' abilities to refine their techniques and strategies.

Today, golf is as much a mental game as it is a physical one, with success often determined by a player's ability to remain calm under pressure and make smart decisions on the course. The evolution of golf reflects not only advancements in technology and technique but also the enduring appeal of a sport that challenges both the body and the mind. As the game continues to grow and develop, it remains a testament to the human desire for precision, competition, and the pursuit of excellence.

WHY LEARN GOLF?

Whether you're a novice, a weekend golfer, or an aspiring professional, taking up golf offers a wealth of benefits that extend far beyond the fairways and greens. Physically, golf enhances hand-eye coordination, improves balance, and promotes flexibility. It's a sport that demands precision and control, requiring both mental acuity and physical dexterity to master the swing, navigate the course, and execute each shot with finesse.

For those seeking a personal challenge, golf presents a

variety of disciplines such as stroke play, match play, and even specialty formats like scramble or skins games, each requiring a unique set of strategies and skills. The sport encourages continuous learning and adaptation, as each round presents new conditions, different courses, and the opportunity to refine your technique.

Beyond the physical advantages, golf builds mental toughness and resilience. The ability to focus on the task at hand, maintain composure under pressure, and persevere through challenges are all vital components of the game. These qualities not only improve your performance on the course but also have practical applications in everyday life. Golf also instills a sense of integrity, sportsmanship, and respect for the rules, as well as for fellow players.

This guide is crafted to take you through the fundamentals of golf. From understanding the basics of club selection and swing mechanics to mastering course management and competition strategies, you'll acquire the comprehensive knowledge needed to elevate your game. Whether your goal is to lower your handicap, enjoy leisurely rounds with friends, or compete at a higher level, this guide will lay the foundation for your success in golf.

Step onto the course and embrace the journey into the world of golf, where each swing tests your skill, every round enhances your strategic thinking, and every day on the links fosters a deeper appreciation for this elegant and challenging sport. Welcome to the world of golf, where precision meets perseverance.

1

THE HISTORY OF GOLF: FROM PASTIME TO PROFESSIONAL SPORT

ORIGINS OF GOLF

Golf boasts a history that stretches back several centuries, evolving from a leisurely pastime into a highly organized and competitive sport enjoyed worldwide. The earliest origins of golf are often debated, but it is widely believed to have developed in Scotland during the Middle Ages, where shepherds would hit stones into rabbit holes using simple clubs. This rudimentary form of the game laid the foundation for what would become the sport of golf.

The formalization of golf began in the 15th century, with the first recorded mention of the game appearing in Scottish documents in 1457, when King James II banned it, fearing it was distracting from military archery practice. Despite this ban, the game continued to grow in popularity, particularly among the Scottish nobility. The establishment of golf clubs, such as the Honorable Company of Edinburgh

Golfers in 1744 and the Royal and Ancient Golf Club of St Andrews in 1754, played a significant role in standardizing the rules and formalizing the sport.

Golf course, Doomdooma, Assam

As golf spread beyond Scotland, it began to take hold in England and later, throughout the British Empire. In the United States, golf gained popularity in the late 19th century, with the formation of the United States Golf Association (USGA) in 1894, which helped standardize the rules and organize competitions across the country.

The modern era of golf emerged in the late 19th and early 20th centuries, driven by advancements in equipment, such as the introduction of the rubber-cored golf ball and the invention of steel-shafted clubs. These innovations, coupled with the establishment of major tournaments like The Open Championship (first played in 1860), The Masters, and the U.S. Open, helped solidify golf's status as a major international sport.

Paris 1900—Golf—Two competitors next to the same hole (cropped)

Today, golf is governed by international bodies such as The R&A and the USGA, which ensure consistency in the rules and fairness in competitions worldwide. The sport includes various formats and disciplines, from stroke play and match play to team events like the Ryder Cup, each with its own unique strategies and challenges. Golf continues to attract players of all ages and abilities, celebrating both individual achievements and the spirit of sportsmanship that defines the game.

THE EVOLUTION OF GOLF: A JOURNEY THROUGH TIME

The Dawn of the Game

Golf, a sport that intertwines precision, strategy, and history, has its roots deeply embedded in the mists of time. The origins of golf are shrouded in legend, with many tracing it back to the rolling hills of Scotland where shepherds, using their crooks, would hit stones into rabbit holes to pass the time. This rudimentary pastime gradually evolved into a structured game, with early forms resembling the golf we know today.

Masonic Golf Balls

By the 15th century, golf had garnered enough popularity in Scotland that King James II famously banned it, fearing it was distracting his soldiers from practicing archery. Despite this, the game persisted, and by the 17th century, it had become a favorite among Scottish nobility. The establishment of the Honorable Company of Edinburgh Golfers in 1744, and the Royal and Ancient Golf Club of St Andrews in 1754, were pivotal in formalizing the rules of the game and establishing golf as a structured sport.

FROM SCOTLAND TO THE WORLD

The game spread beyond the borders of Scotland, taking root in England and later across the British Empire. The first recorded international match was held in 1682 between Scotland and England, symbolizing golf's growing popularity. As the game expanded, so did the need for standardized rules and equipment, which were largely developed by the Royal and Ancient Golf Club of St Andrews.

Tony Jacklin's golf ball from Royal Birkdale, 1969

Golf made its way to the United States in the late 19th century, where it quickly gained popularity. The formation of the United States Golf Association (USGA) in 1894 was instrumental in standardizing the game in America, helping to set the stage for the establishment of iconic tournaments such as the U.S. Open.

THE MODERNISATION OF GOLF

The 20th century saw significant advancements in golf, both in terms of technology and international competition. The introduction of the rubber-cored ball in the early 1900s revolutionized the game, offering greater control and distance. Similarly, the development of steel-shafted clubs in the 1920s allowed for more consistent and powerful swings, forever changing the way the game was played.

Golf's appeal broadened with the establishment of major tournaments like The Open Championship, The Masters, and the PGA Championship. These events not only brought together the best golfers from around the world but also helped to popularize the sport among the general public. Players like Bobby Jones, who won the Grand Slam in 1930, became household names, inspiring a new generation of golfers.

INTERNATIONAL EXPANSION AND TECHNOLOGICAL ADVANCEMENTS

The post-war era marked a period of rapid international expansion for golf. The rise of televised tournaments in the 1950s and 60s brought the sport into living rooms around the world, increasing its popularity and accessibility.

Featherie golf balls

The Ryder Cup, which pits teams from Europe and the United States against each other, became a symbol of international golf competition, showcasing the sport's growing global appeal.

Technological advancements continued to shape the game, with innovations such as graphite shafts and cavity-back irons allowing for greater forgiveness and accuracy. The introduction of electronic scoring systems and advanced training techniques further elevated the level of play, making golf more competitive and engaging.

LEGENDARY GOLFERS AND ICONIC TOURNAMENTS

Throughout its storied history, golf has produced some of the most revered and celebrated athletes in the world of sport. These golfers have not only dominated their respective eras but have also inspired generations of players with their remarkable achievements, consistency, and dedication to the game.

One of the most iconic figures in the history of golf is **Jack Nicklaus**, often referred to as "The Golden Bear." Widely regarded as the greatest golfer of all time, Nicklaus won a record 18 major championships, including six Masters titles, five PGA Championships, four U.S. Opens, and three Open Championships. Known for his extraordinary mental toughness and strategic play, Nicklaus's career spanned over three decades, during which he consistently demonstrated the precision and composure needed to succeed at the highest levels of the game.

Another legendary golfer is **Tiger Woods**, whose impact on the sport is unparalleled in the modern era. Bursting onto the scene with his 12-stroke victory at the 1997 Masters, Woods has since won 15 major championships, including five Masters titles and three U.S. Opens. His combination of power, finesse, and competitive drive revolutionized the game, drawing millions of new fans and inspiring a generation of young golfers. Woods's ability to perform under immense pressure and his numerous record-breaking performances have solidified his status as a global sports icon.

1921 Leeds Cup Golf Championship Winners Medal

Arnold Palmer, known as "The King," was not only a great golfer but also a charismatic ambassador for the sport. With seven major championships to his name, Palmer's aggressive playing style and magnetic personality helped popularize golf during the 1950s and 60s, especially with the advent of televised tournaments. His legacy lives on through the Arnold Palmer Invitational, a key event on the PGA Tour, and the countless fans he inspired throughout his career.

Seve Ballesteros of Spain was another golfer who left an indelible mark on the sport. A master of the short game and a wizard around the greens, Ballesteros won five major championships, including three Open Championships and two Masters titles. His flair, creativity, and passion for the game made him a beloved figure in Europe and around the world. Ballesteros was instrumental in revitalizing the Ryder Cup, leading Europe to several victories and establishing the event as one of the most fiercely contested in golf.

In addition to these legends, golf has seen countless other greats who have shaped the sport's history. **Gary Player**, one of golf's most successful international players, won nine major championships and became known for his rigorous fitness regimen and global impact on the game. **Ben Hogan**, revered for his precision and dedication, overcame a life-threatening car accident to win nine major titles, including three in a single year—1953. **Tom Watson** dominated the Open Championship, winning five titles in a career that spanned over three decades.

Golf's rich history is also defined by its iconic tournaments, each with its own traditions and prestige. **The Masters Tournament**, held annually at Augusta National Golf Club, is perhaps the most famous of all, known for its lush green fairways, azalea-lined holes, and the coveted Green Jacket awarded to the winner. **The Open Championship**, often referred to as the British Open, is the oldest of the four majors, played on some of the most challenging links courses in the UK. **The U.S. Open** is renowned for its tough course setups, demanding accuracy and mental resilience from the players, while **The PGA Championship** has a reputation for attracting the strongest field in golf.

1921 Leeds Cup Medal: Professional Golfers' Association Insignia

Beyond these majors, the **Ryder Cup** stands out as one of the most exciting and prestigious events in the sport. This biennial competition between teams from Europe and the United States is celebrated for its intense atmosphere, passionate fan base, and the camaraderie and rivalry it fosters among players.

Golf has also seen significant contributions from players outside the traditional powerhouses of the sport. **Annika Sörenstam** from Sweden is widely regarded as the greatest female golfer of all time, with 10 major championships and 72 LPGA Tour victories. **Lorena Ochoa** of Mexico dominated women's golf in the 2000s, becoming the world number one and winning two major championships before retiring at the peak of her career.

In India, **Jeev Milkha Singh** has been a trailblazer for the sport, becoming the first Indian golfer to break into the top 50 of the Official World Golf Ranking and winning multiple titles on the European and Asian Tours. His success has paved the way for other Indian golfers like **Anirban Lahiri** and **Shubhankar Sharma**, who have continued to elevate India's presence in the international golf scene.

These golfers, along with many others, have not only achieved greatness on the course but have also contributed to the sport's growth and global appeal. Their dedication, sportsmanship, and remarkable accomplishments continue to inspire new generations of golfers, ensuring that the legacy of this ancient game endures for years to come.

THE IMPACT OF GOLF ON SOCIETY

Thomas William Marshall - médaille Société de Golf de Paris 1902

In countries like Scotland, where golf originated, the sport is not just a pastime but a cultural institution. It has played a significant role in shaping national identity and pride, with iconic courses such as St Andrews considered hallowed ground for golfers worldwide. The international appeal of golf is further demonstrated by its inclusion in the Olympic Games, where it showcases the sport's global reach and the high level of skill required to compete at the highest levels.

Golf also plays an essential role in environmental stewardship. Many modern golf courses are designed with sustainability in mind, incorporating natural landscapes and promoting biodiversity. The sport encourages respect for the environment, as players must navigate and appreciate the natural elements that make up a course. This connection to nature is one of the many aspects that draw people to the game, offering a form of physical exercise that is both challenging and rejuvenating.

Despite the challenges that golf faces, including concerns about accessibility, the cost of participation, and the environmental impact of maintaining courses, the sport's positive contributions to society are undeniable. Golf promotes healthy living, as it combines physical activity with time spent outdoors. It also contributes to local economies, particularly in regions where golf tourism is a significant industry. The sport's ability to adapt and evolve, embracing new technologies and sustainability practices, ensures its continued relevance in the modern world.

Gold, silver and bronze medals for World Adventure Golf Masters in Kungälv, Sweden, 2019

The impact of golf on youth development is another critical aspect of its societal contribution. Junior golf programs around the world focus on teaching young players not only the technical aspects of the game but also the importance of discipline, respect, and perseverance. These programs often emphasize the values of fair play, honesty, and integrity—principles that young golfers carry with them both on and off the course. As these young players mature, they become ambassadors for the sport, promoting its values and encouraging the next generation to take up the game.

In conclusion, golf's influence on society is both deep and enduring. The sport has the power to shape individuals, foster communities, and contribute to the broader social and economic fabric. As golf continues to evolve, it will undoubtedly remain a symbol of excellence, tradition, and the pursuit of personal and collective achievement. Its role in promoting values such as patience, respect, and environmental stewardship ensures that golf will continue to inspire and unite people around the world for generations to come.

Ball flight laws

SECTION ONE

GETTING STARTED

2

UNDERSTANDING GOLF: THE ART OF THE GAME

WHAT IS GOLF?

Golf is a sport that combines precision, strategy, and a deep connection with the natural environment. It is a game where players use a variety of clubs to hit a small ball into a series of holes on a course, doing so in as few strokes as possible. Unlike many other sports that rely on speed, strength, or physical contact, golf is a test of finesse, mental endurance, and tactical planning. It's a unique blend of physical skill and mental acuity, where the objective is not just to play against opponents but also to challenge oneself and the course.

The essence of golf lies in its simplicity: to complete each hole in the least number of strokes. However, achieving this requires mastering a range of techniques, including a proper grip, stance, and swing. Each of these elements must be perfectly coordinated to achieve accuracy and distance, making golf as much a game of skill as it is of strategy.

Whether you are driving off the tee, hitting an approach shot to the green, or sinking a putt, every aspect of your game requires careful thought and precise execution.

Hickory golfstokken

THE ENVIRONMENT OF THE GAME

Golf is played on courses that vary greatly in design, each presenting its own set of challenges. These courses can range from the rolling fairways of a parkland course to the rugged, wind-swept dunes of a links course. The diversity of course layouts means that no two rounds of golf are ever the same, as players must adapt their strategy and shot selection to the unique conditions of each course.

The course itself is divided into different areas, including the teeing ground, fairway, rough, and putting green, each demanding different approaches and techniques. For instance, the smooth, closely-mown fairway is ideal for long, accurate shots, while the rough, with its longer grass, presents a greater challenge, requiring more power and control. The green, where the hole is located, is where the final strokes of a hole are played, often demanding a delicate touch and a keen eye for reading the slope and speed of the surface.

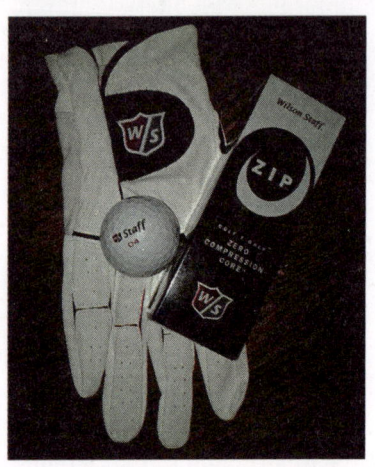

Misc. Wilson Staff golf equipment, including golf glove, ZIPI golf ball, sleeve of ZIP golf balls

THE PRECISION AND STRATEGY OF GOLF

Precision in golf is not just about hitting the ball; it's about hitting it well. This means that every aspect of your swing—from the backswing to the follow-through—must be carefully calibrated to ensure the ball travels in the intended direction and distance. Even the slightest deviation in angle or force can result in the ball veering off course, leading to missed opportunities and higher scores.

UNDERSTANDING GOLF: THE ART OF THE GAME

ASICS's wood clubs for Ground Golf and balls in Japan

Strategically, golf is a game of decisions. Players must constantly assess their position on the course, the conditions, and their own abilities to choose the best course of action. This might involve deciding whether to play aggressively with a driver off the tee or conservatively with an iron, whether to aim directly at the flag or to play safe to avoid hazards, or how to approach a tricky putt. Each decision carries risk and reward, making golf a cerebral sport as much as a physical one.

THE CHALLENGE OF THE COURSE

Courses are designed to test a golfer's skill, patience, and creativity. Hazards such as bunkers, water bodies, and out-of-bounds areas are strategically placed to challenge players and force them to think critically about each shot. Wind, weather, and terrain also play significant roles in shaping the difficulty of a course, requiring players to adapt and make adjustments on the fly.

Moreover, the mental aspect of golf is as challenging as the physical. Maintaining focus, managing nerves, and staying calm under pressure are essential to success. The ability to recover from a bad shot and keep a positive mindset can often make the difference between a good round and a great one. In competitive play, where the stakes are high and the margins for error are slim, the mental game becomes even more crucial.

GOLF AS A LIFELONG PURSUIT

Golf is more than just a sport; it's a lifelong journey of learning and self-improvement. Whether you are a beginner learning the basics or an experienced player honing your skills, golf offers endless opportunities for growth. The sport's unique combination of physical precision, mental strategy, and connection with nature makes it a deeply rewarding experience.

As golfers continue to play and refine their techniques, they develop a deeper understanding of the game and themselves. Every round of golf presents new challenges and lessons, making it a sport that continuously tests and rewards those who are committed to improving.

In conclusion, golf is a sport that demands precision, strategy, and mental resilience. It is a game where every stroke counts and where success is measured not just by scores but by the personal satisfaction of overcoming challenges and achieving one's goals. Whether played competitively or for leisure, golf is a sport that offers something for everyone, making it a truly unique and enduring pursuit.

Junior left-handed golf clubs

THE ESSENTIAL RULES AND REGULATIONS OF GOLF

1. The Golf Course

Golf is a game defined by its environment, with each course offering a unique blend of challenges and beauty. A standard golf course consists of 18 holes, each with its own fairway, hazards, and green. The layout and design of these courses vary greatly, with elements such as bunkers, water hazards, and undulating greens adding layers of complexity. Courses can be broadly categorized into parkland, links, and desert courses, each with distinct characteristics that influence play. Understanding the nuances of different course types is essential for golfers looking to adapt their strategies and refine their skills.

Golf club, Ping G10 24° hybrid – II

The fairways and greens must be meticulously maintained to ensure a consistent playing surface. The tees, fairways, rough, and greens are all carefully manicured to provide a variety of playing conditions. Bunkers, water hazards, and out-of-bounds areas add to the complexity, requiring golfers to employ both skill and strategy. Golfers must be aware of local rules specific to each course, which can influence play significantly, such as rules about which areas are considered ground under repair or how certain hazards are treated.

2. Distances and Targets

In golf, precision is paramount. Distances vary from hole to hole, with par-3 holes generally ranging from 100 to 250 yards, par-4s from 250 to 450 yards, and par-5s extending beyond 450 yards. The objective is to play each hole in as few strokes as possible, aiming to finish with a score that matches or beats the course's par. The par score represents the number of strokes an expert golfer is expected to take to complete the hole.

Golf club, Callaway X-20 4 iron

The targets in golf—the holes themselves—are placed in greens that vary in size and slope. Greens are typically designed to test the golfer's putting ability, with subtle undulations and varying speeds making each putt a challenge. The hole, marked by a flagstick, is 4.25 inches in diameter, and the objective is to sink the ball into the hole with as few strokes as possible. On approach shots, golfers aim for specific areas of the green to give themselves the best chance of making the next putt.

3. Scoring

Golf is scored by counting the number of strokes taken to complete each hole. The total number of strokes for all holes is the player's score for the round. A typical scoring system includes terms such as birdie (one stroke under par), par (equal to par), bogey (one stroke over par), and so on. The fewer strokes a player takes, the better their score.

In match play, scoring is done on a hole-by-hole basis, with the winner being the player who wins the most holes. Stroke play, on the other hand, counts the total number of strokes taken over the entire round, with the lowest total winning. In tournament play, the cut-off after the first two rounds determines which players will continue in the competition, based on their scores relative to the field.

4. Tiebreakers and Playoffs

In the event of a tie in professional golf tournaments, a playoff is often used to determine the winner. The format of the playoff can vary, with some tournaments employing sudden death, where the first player to win a hole outright is declared the winner. Others use aggregate score playoffs over a set number of holes. The pressure during these moments is immense, requiring players to perform at their best under high stakes.

Playoffs highlight the mental toughness and composure of the golfers, as they often face the most challenging holes in front of a global audience. The ability to maintain focus and execute under pressure is what often separates the great from the good in golf.

5. Penalties and Infractions

Golf is a game of honor and sportsmanship, with strict rules governing play. Common penalties include one-stroke penalties for lost balls or out-of-bounds shots, two-stroke penalties for incorrect play, and disqualification for serious breaches of the rules. For example, if a golfer accidentally moves their ball in play, they must add a penalty stroke and replace the ball to its original position.

Penalties also apply to equipment infractions, such as carrying more than 14 clubs in the bag or using non-conforming equipment. Competitors are expected to know

UNDERSTANDING GOLF: THE ART OF THE GAME

and adhere to these rules, as ignorance is not considered an excuse. The Rules of Golf, as governed by The R&A and the USGA, provides the definitive guide to the sport's regulations.

6. Equipment Standards

Golfers are required to use equipment that conforms to standards set by the governing bodies of the sport. This includes the clubs, balls, and any other equipment used during play. For instance, the maximum number of clubs a player can carry is 14, and each club must meet specific criteria in terms of length, weight, and face angle. The ball must also conform to size and weight regulations, and any modifications to equipment must adhere to the rules.

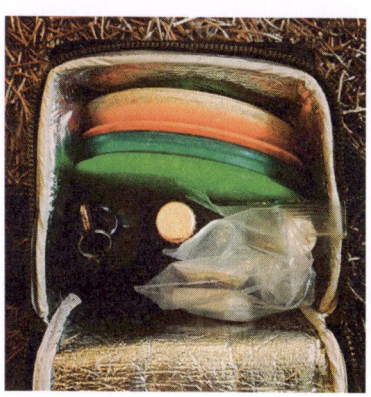

A putter, driver, and two midranges; a bottled water, Dogfish Head, and some 35 SPF sunscreen

Players often customize their equipment to suit their playing style, such as adjusting the loft of their clubs or selecting balls that offer specific spin characteristics.

However, all modifications must comply with the standards to ensure fair play.

7. The Role of Officials

In golf, referees and rules officials play a crucial role in ensuring that the game is played fairly and within the rules. They are responsible for interpreting the rules, resolving disputes, and maintaining the integrity of the competition. During tournaments, they are present on the course to oversee play, answer rule queries, and enforce penalties when necessary.

Officials are also tasked with monitoring the pace of play, ensuring that players adhere to the time limits for completing each hole. In professional golf, slow play can lead to penalties, including stroke penalties or even disqualification, highlighting the importance of playing efficiently and within the allotted time.

THE ROLE OF GOLF ORGANIZATIONS (R&A, USGA, PGA, ETC.)

Golf is a sport that thrives on its traditions, values, and the adherence to a structured set of rules and regulations. The sport is governed by several major organizations, each playing a crucial role in maintaining the integrity, fairness, and global reach of golf. These bodies not only establish the standards and rules for the sport but also work to promote golf, ensuring its growth and accessibility around the world. The most prominent organizations in the golfing world include The R&A, the United States Golf Association (USGA), the Professional Golfers' Association (PGA), and

UNDERSTANDING GOLF: THE ART OF THE GAME

the European Tour. These organizations are indispensable in maintaining the sport's structure, providing a framework for competition, and nurturing talent at all levels.

Ranges and Clubhouse

1. The R&A

The R&A, formed in 2004 but with roots dating back to the 18th century as part of the Royal and Ancient Golf Club of St Andrews, is one of the oldest and most prestigious governing bodies in golf. It oversees the rules of golf outside the United States and Mexico, working in collaboration with the USGA to produce the Rules of Golf, which govern the sport worldwide. The R&A is responsible for organizing The Open Championship, one of the four major golf tournaments, and is a key player in setting the standards for amateur and professional golf.

The R&A also focuses on the development and promotion of golf globally, particularly in emerging markets. It invests in grassroots initiatives, junior golf programs, and the sustainability of the sport, ensuring that golf continues to thrive in the modern era. The organization's commitment to inclusivity is evident in its efforts to make the game more accessible to people of all ages and backgrounds, while its governance ensures that the traditions and integrity of golf are preserved.

2. United States Golf Association (USGA)

Established in 1894, the USGA is the governing body for golf in the United States and Mexico. Alongside The R&A, the USGA plays a pivotal role in maintaining the Rules of Golf, ensuring consistency and fairness in how the game is played globally. The USGA is also responsible for conducting some of the most prestigious golf tournaments in the world, including the U.S. Open, the U.S. Women's Open, and the U.S. Senior Open.

Caddyrack Prototypes

In addition to overseeing the rules and organizing major championships, the USGA is deeply involved in the research and development of golf equipment standards, working to ensure that technological advancements do not undermine the skill-based nature of the game. The organization also focuses on environmental sustainability, promoting practices that reduce the ecological footprint of golf courses across the country.

3. Professional Golfers' Association (PGA)

The PGA, with its various branches such as the PGA of America and the PGA Tour, is primarily focused on the professional side of golf. Founded in 1916, the PGA of America is one of the largest sports organizations in the world, representing the interests of over 28,000 golf professionals. It is responsible for organizing major events like the PGA Championship and the Ryder Cup, which pits top players from the United States against their European counterparts.

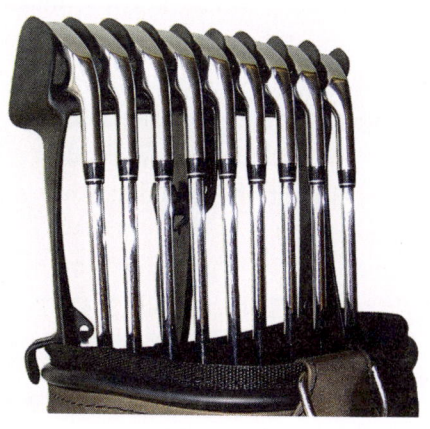

Caddyrack 9 slot rack Installed in a Golf Bag

The PGA Tour, established in 1968, manages professional golf tours in the United States, including the PGA Tour, the Korn Ferry Tour, and the PGA Tour Champions. These tours provide a platform for the world's best golfers to compete at the highest level, offering significant prize money and global exposure. The PGA also plays a crucial role in the development of young talent, providing training and certification for golf instructors and professionals.

4. European Tour

The European Tour, founded in 1972, is the principal professional golf tour in Europe. It oversees three main tours: the European Tour, the European Senior Tour, and the Challenge Tour, which serves as a developmental tour for up-and-coming golfers. The European Tour has been instrumental in popularizing golf across Europe, bringing the sport to a wider audience and creating opportunities for golfers from various backgrounds to compete internationally.

The European Tour is also known for its innovative approach to tournament formats, including the introduction of the Rolex Series, which features some of the most prestigious and lucrative events on the tour. The organization collaborates closely with the PGA Tour to co-sanction events and maintain a global calendar that showcases the best of professional golf.

DISCIPLINES AND CATEGORIES IN GOLF

1. Stroke Play

Stroke play is the most common format in golf, where the total number of strokes taken over a round or series of rounds determines the winner. This discipline requires players to complete the course in the fewest strokes possible. The consistency and precision required in stroke play are paramount, as every shot counts towards the final score. This format is used in major tournaments such as The Open Championship and the U.S. Open, where the pressure to perform across multiple rounds can test even the most seasoned professionals. Stroke play rewards players who can maintain focus, manage their game across different conditions, and handle the mental pressure of a cumulative score.

2. Match Play

Match play is a direct competition between two golfers, where the objective is to win individual holes rather than counting the total number of strokes. This head-to-head format adds a strategic element to the game, as players can focus on beating their opponent on each hole rather than worrying about their overall score. The dynamic of match play allows for aggressive strategies and the opportunity to recover from mistakes more easily than in stroke play. Competitions like the Ryder Cup and the World Match Play Championship highlights the intensity and tactical nature of this format.

3. Skins Game

The Skins Game is a popular format where each hole is assigned a monetary or point value, and the golfer with the lowest score on that hole wins the "skin." If two or more players tie, the skin carries over to the next hole. This format encourages risk-taking and aggressive play, as the stakes can increase significantly as the round progresses. The Skins

Game is often used in charity events and exhibitions, where the entertainment value is as important as the competition itself. The format's unpredictability and potential for large rewards on single holes make it an exciting variation of traditional golf.

4. Stableford

Stableford is a scoring system where points are awarded based on the number of strokes taken relative to par on each hole. Unlike stroke play, where the total number of strokes determines the score, Stableford rewards players for better-than-average play and penalizes less for poor holes. This format encourages attacking play and reduces the impact of a few bad holes on the overall score. Stableford competitions are popular in amateur events, where the focus is on enjoyment and participation rather than strict competition.

5. Fourball and Foursomes

Fourball and Foursomes are team formats commonly used in events like the Ryder Cup and Presidents Cup. In Fourball, each player in a two-person team plays their ball, and the team's score for each hole is the lower of the two players' scores. Foursomes, on the other hand, involves two players alternating shots with the same ball, providing a unique test of teamwork and strategy. These formats require strong communication and trust between partners, as each player must adapt their game to complement their teammate's strengths and weaknesses. The combination of individual skill and team dynamics makes these formats both challenging and exciting.

6. Scramble

The Scramble format is popular in casual and charity tournaments, where teams of two or more players each hit a tee shot, then select the best shot and continue play from that spot. This process repeats until the ball is holed. The Scramble is a more relaxed format that emphasizes teamwork and collective strategy, allowing players of varying skill levels to contribute to the team's success. This format is ideal for social events and fundraisers, where the focus is on fun and camaraderie rather than intense competition.

7. Par-3 Courses and Pitch and Putt

Par-3 courses and Pitch and Putt offer a shorter, more accessible version of golf, focusing primarily on short-game skills. These courses typically feature holes that are all par-3s, with distances ranging from 100 to 200 yards. Pitch and Putt is an even shorter variant, with holes generally less than 100 yards. These formats are perfect for beginners or those looking to refine their approach shots and putting. They provide a quick and enjoyable way to play golf, emphasizing accuracy and finesse over power.

8. Long Drive Competitions

Long Drive competitions focus solely on distance, with golfers competing to hit the ball as far as possible. While this discipline emphasizes power and technique in driving, it also requires precision to keep the ball within designated boundaries. Long Drive events are thrilling to watch and participate in, showcasing the explosive power and athleticism of golfers. Competitors must balance raw strength with control, as accuracy is just as important as distance in this format.

EQUIPMENT AND SAFETY STANDARDS IN GOLF

Golf, much like shooting sports, demands a precise understanding of equipment and a strict adherence to safety standards to ensure the well-being of players, officials, and spectators. Whether you're a seasoned professional or a novice, being well-versed in the equipment used and the safety protocols followed is essential for enjoying and excelling in the game of golf.

1. Golf Clubs and Balls

The choice of golf clubs and balls is critical to performance and is tailored to the specific needs and preferences of each player. A standard golf bag can carry up to 14 clubs, which typically include a mix of drivers, woods, irons, wedges, and a putter. Each club is designed for specific types of shots, with varying degrees of loft, shaft flexibility, and head design to optimize performance in different situations. For instance, drivers are used for long-distance shots off the tee, while wedges are essential for precision shots around the green.

Golf balls are equally important, with their construction influencing spin, distance, and control. Modern golf balls usually feature a multi-layer design that balances distance with feel. The dimples on a golf ball are engineered to reduce air resistance and increase lift, contributing to longer and more accurate shots. Adhering to the standards set by governing bodies like the USGA and The R&A ensures fairness and consistency in play.

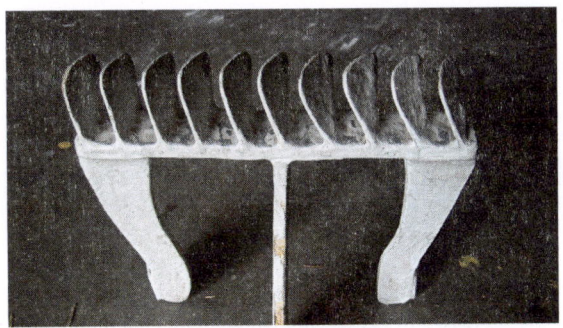

This is the first Caddyrack Prototype made from Balsa and Foam in 1993

2. Protective Gear and Apparel

While golf is generally considered a low-risk sport, protective gear and appropriate apparel are essential for comfort and safety on the course. Golfers often wear gloves to improve grip and prevent blisters, particularly during long rounds. Sunglasses and hats are commonly used to protect against sun exposure, which is crucial given the outdoor nature of the sport.

Footwear is another critical aspect, with golf shoes designed to provide stability, especially on uneven terrain. Modern golf shoes often feature spiked or spikeless soles to improve traction, which is vital when swinging a club. Proper attire, including moisture-wicking clothing and rain gear, ensures that golfers can perform comfortably in various weather conditions.

3. Safety Protocols

Golf, while leisurely, is not without its hazards. Strict safety protocols are in place to protect players, caddies, and spectators. These protocols include maintaining awareness of other players on the course, ensuring that no one is in the line of a swing or shot, and adhering to the pace of play to prevent bottlenecks and accidents.

Golfers are trained to shout "Fore!" as a warning if a ball is headed towards another person, and courses are designed with safety in mind, including designated areas for spectators and clearly marked hazards. Additionally, players must be cautious of environmental factors such as weather, particularly lightning, which can pose significant risks. Courses often have warning systems and protocols in place for such conditions, ensuring the safety of all participants.

4. Course Safety and Layout

Golf courses are meticulously designed to provide both a challenging and safe environment for players. The layout of a course includes various hazards, such as bunkers, water features, and roughs, which add complexity to the game but must also be navigated safely. Course designers consider factors like fairway width, green size, and the placement of hazards to ensure a fair test of skill while maintaining safety.

Maintenance of the course is critical, with regular checks to ensure that the playing surface is free of debris and hazards that could cause injury. Greenskeepers and maintenance staff play a crucial role in this process, ensuring that bunkers are raked, greens are mown, and fairways are clear. The design also incorporates features like cart paths and signage to direct players safely around the course.

UNDERSTANDING GOLF: THE ART OF THE GAME

3 golf clubs and ball at Wakasu Golf Links, Tokyo

5. Marshals and Course Officials

Course marshals and officials are integral to the smooth and safe operation of a golf event. These individuals are responsible for maintaining order on the course, enforcing the rules, and ensuring that play proceeds in a timely and safe manner. They have the authority to manage the pace of play, intervene in disputes, and enforce penalties for rule violations.

3

ESSENTIAL EQUIPMENT AND GEAR FOR GOLF ENTHUSIASTS

MASTERING THE TOOLS OF THE GAME: CLUBS, BALLS, ATTIRE, AND MORE

Golf is a sport that demands precision, skill, and the right equipment. The proper gear not only enhances your performance on the course but also ensures comfort and compliance with the game's regulations. In this comprehensive guide, we'll delve into the essential equipment for golfers, offering insights on choosing, maintaining, and utilizing each piece of gear effectively.

1. Golf Clubs: The Core of Your Game

Purpose and Importance

Golf clubs are the fundamental tools of the game, designed for a variety of shots ranging from long drives to delicate putts. Selecting the right set of clubs tailored to your play style is crucial for achieving optimal performance on the course.

Types of Golf Clubs:

- **Drivers:** Typically used for long-distance shots off the tee, drivers have larger heads and longer shafts to maximize distance.
- **Fairway Woods:** Ideal for longer shots from the fairway, these clubs offer a balance of distance and control.
- **Irons:** Available in numbered sets, irons are versatile and used for various shots, including approach shots and tee shots on shorter holes.
- **Wedges:** Specialized irons like pitching wedges and sand wedges are designed for short, high-loft shots, including bunker play.
- **Putters:** Used on the green, putters are designed to roll the ball smoothly into the hole with precision.

Choosing the Right Golf Clubs:

- **Fit and Comfort:** The club should feel comfortable in your hands, with a shaft length and grip size that suit your physical dimensions and swing style.
- **Purpose:** Different clubs are suited for various situations on the course. Ensure your set includes a range of clubs for versatility.
- **Quality and Brand:** Invest in reputable brands known for durability and performance. Clubs from trusted manufacturers offer better control and consistency.

2. Golf Balls: Precision in Every Shot

Purpose and Importance

The golf ball is your primary point of contact with the course. Its design and construction significantly affect your distance, control, and overall performance.

Types of Golf Balls:

- **Two-Piece Balls:** Known for durability and distance, these are ideal for beginners and high-handicap golfers.
- **Multi-Layered Balls:** Designed for more experienced players, these balls offer a balance of distance and control, with better spin and feel around the greens.
- **Low-Compression Balls:** Suited for golfers with slower swing speeds, these balls provide more distance and a softer feel.

Choosing the Right Golf Ball:

- **Compatibility:** Select a ball that complements your swing speed and playing style.
- **Performance Needs:** Consider whether you prioritize distance, control, or spin, and choose a ball that meets those requirements.
- **Quality:** Premium balls from established brands offer consistent performance and durability, especially for competitive play.

3. Golf Attire: Comfort Meets Functionality

Purpose and Importance

Proper golf attire not only meets the dress codes of most courses but also ensures you remain comfortable throughout your round. The right clothing allows for freedom of movement and protection against varying weather conditions.

Types of Golf Attire:

- **Shirts:** Polo shirts are the standard, offering breathability and a professional appearance.

- **Trousers and Shorts:** Lightweight and flexible materials like polyester blends are ideal, providing comfort without restricting movement.
- **Shoes:** Golf shoes with spikes or soft cleats ensure stability and traction on the course, while being comfortable for long walks.
- **Outerwear:** Waterproof jackets and windbreakers are essential for adverse weather, ensuring you stay dry and maintain flexibility.

Choosing the Right Golf Attire:

- **Fit and Mobility:** Clothing should allow a full range of motion without being too tight or too loose.
- **Weather Appropriateness:** Dress in layers for changing weather conditions, including moisture-wicking fabrics for hot days and insulated options for cooler rounds.
- **Style and Compliance:** Ensure your attire meets the course's dress code while reflecting your personal style.

4. Golf Accessories: The Unsung Heroes

Purpose and Importance

Accessories may seem secondary, but they play a vital role in enhancing your performance and experience on the course.

Essential Golf Accessories:

- **Gloves:** A good golf glove improves grip and prevents blisters, especially on hot days. Leather gloves offer excellent feel, while synthetic options are more durable.
- **Tees:** Available in various heights and materials, tees are essential for the perfect setup on the tee box.

- **Ball Markers:** Used to mark your ball's position on the green, these small tools are a must-have for every golfer.
- **Divot Repair Tools:** These help maintain the condition of the greens by allowing you to repair pitch marks made by your ball.
- **Rangefinders and GPS Devices:** These gadgets help you measure distances on the course, improving shot accuracy and course management.

Choosing the Right Accessories:

- **Functionality:** Choose accessories that enhance your game, such as gloves that provide a secure grip or tees that suit your driving style.
- **Durability:** Invest in high-quality accessories that can withstand regular use and the elements.
- **Convenience:** Select items that are easy to carry and store in your golf bag, ensuring they are always within reach when needed.

5. Golf Bags and Carts: Organization on the Course

Purpose and Importance

A well-organized golf bag ensures that all your equipment is protected and easily accessible, while a sturdy cart helps transport your gear around the course with ease.

Types of Golf Bags:

- **Carry Bags:** Lightweight and designed for those who prefer to walk the course. These often come with dual straps for even weight distribution.
- **Cart Bags:** Heavier and designed to sit on a golf cart.

They offer more storage and easier access to your clubs and accessories.
- **Stand Bags:** Equipped with built-in legs, these bags can stand upright on the course, offering convenience and easy access to your clubs.

Choosing the Right Golf Bag:

- **Size and Weight:** Ensure the bag fits all your clubs comfortably while being light enough to carry or transport.
- **Storage Capacity:** Look for a bag with ample pockets for your balls, tees, gloves, and other accessories.
- **Durability:** Choose a bag made from strong, water-resistant materials to protect your gear in all weather conditions.

Golf Carts:

- **Manual Push/Pull Carts:** Ideal for those who prefer walking but want to save energy. Look for lightweight, foldable models for easy storage.
- **Electric Carts:** These offer the ultimate convenience, carrying your bag for you and often featuring remote control capabilities.

6. Maintenance Tools: Keeping Your Gear in Top Shape

Purpose and Importance

Regular maintenance of your golf equipment ensures it performs at its best and extends its lifespan. Cleaning and care tools are essential for keeping your clubs, balls, and other gear in top condition.

Essential Maintenance Tools:

- **Club Cleaners:** Brushes and towels designed to clean the grooves of your clubs, ensuring they maintain optimal spin and control.
- **Ball Cleaners:** Portable devices or towels that remove dirt and grass from your golf balls, ensuring they fly true.
- **Shoe Cleaners:** Brushes and wipes that keep your golf shoes free of mud and debris, preserving their grip and appearance.

Maintaining Your Golf Equipment:

- **Regular Cleaning:** Clean your clubs and balls after each round to prevent the buildup of dirt and grime, which can affect performance.
- **Storage:** Store your equipment in a dry, cool place to prevent rust and deterioration, particularly during the off-season.
- **Inspection:** Routinely check your gear for signs of wear and tear, and replace any damaged items to ensure optimal performance.

By investing in the right golf equipment and taking care of it, you'll not only enhance your performance but also enjoy the game to its fullest. Each piece of gear plays a crucial role in your overall golfing experience, so choose wisely, maintain diligently, and play confidently.

4

GOLF STANCE AND MOVEMENT: MASTERING THE FOUNDATION OF THE GAME

GOLF, MUCH LIKE SHOOTING SPORTS, IS ABOUT FAR more than simply hitting the ball; it requires a blend of precision, strategy, and fluid movement. Central to mastering the game of golf is understanding the importance of a solid stance and effective movement. This chapter provides a comprehensive guide to golf stances, their significance, and detailed movement techniques that are essential for both the driving range and the golf course.

THE IMPORTANCE OF A SOLID STANCE

A golfer's stance is the foundation of their swing, stability, and overall performance. A proper stance not only supports shot accuracy but also influences the ability to generate power, control the ball's trajectory, and maintain balance throughout the round. Here's a closer look at why a solid stance is essential:

- **Stability and Balance:** A well-established stance ensures that the golfer remains balanced and stable, even when executing complex shots or swinging under pressure. The stance distributes weight evenly, allowing the golfer to maintain a low center of gravity, which is critical for maintaining swing plane consistency and delivering powerful, controlled shots.

Golfball on the fairway and green

- **Accuracy and Consistency:** A consistent stance helps golfers develop muscle memory, allowing for more precise and repeatable swings. By anchoring the body in a reliable position, golfers can focus on the finer points of the swing, such as clubface alignment and impact position, rather than compensating for imbalance or movement.
- **Power Generation:** Proper stance and body positioning are crucial for maximizing power, especially in driving. By positioning the body to leverage the ground effectively, golfers can generate greater clubhead speed, leading to longer drives and more powerful iron shots.

- **Endurance and Comfort:** In golf, especially during lengthy rounds or tournaments, maintaining a comfortable and sustainable stance is vital. A proper stance reduces fatigue, allowing the golfer to perform consistently over time and maintain focus on every shot.

BASIC GOLF STANCES: SQUARE, OPEN, AND CLOSED STANCES

In golf, there are several fundamental stances, each with its own unique advantages and suitable applications depending on the type of shot, the club used, and personal preference.

SQUARE STANCE

- **Description:** The square stance is the most commonly used in golf, where the feet are positioned parallel to the target line, with the shoulders, hips, and feet all aligned square to the target. The golfer's weight is distributed evenly across both feet, with knees slightly flexed for flexibility and balance.
- **Advantages:**
  - *Consistency and Control:* This stance provides a straightforward approach, ensuring that the golfer's body remains aligned with the target throughout the swing, enhancing accuracy.
  - *Power and Distance:* The balanced weight distribution and alignment facilitate a powerful rotation, essential for generating distance, particularly with drivers and long irons.
  - *Versatility:* The square stance is suitable for most

shots, from tee shots to approach shots, making it a fundamental stance for all golfers.
- **Applications:** Commonly used across all levels of play, the square stance is particularly favored for full swings, as it promotes consistency and power.

OPEN STANCE

- **Description:** In the open stance, the golfer's front foot (closest to the target) is pulled back slightly, creating an open position relative to the target line. The hips and shoulders follow the alignment of the feet, resulting in an open position.
- **Advantages:**
  - *Shot Shaping:* This stance allows for easier execution of fade shots (left-to-right for right-handed golfers), as the open position promotes an out-to-in swing path.
  - *Flexibility in Bunker Play:* The open stance is often used in greenside bunker shots, as it allows for better control of the sand wedge's face angle and a softer, higher trajectory.
  - *Improved Vision:* By opening the stance, golfers can see the target line more clearly, which can improve alignment and confidence.
- **Applications:** The open stance is commonly used for shots that require shaping the ball or for short game scenarios where precision and spin control are paramount.

CLOSED STANCE

- **Description:** In the closed stance, the golfer's back foot (farthest from the target) is pulled back slightly, creating a closed position relative to the target line. The hips and shoulders follow the alignment of the feet, resulting in a closed position.
- **Advantages:**
  - *Shot Shaping:* This stance favors drawing the ball (right-to-left for right-handed golfers), as it promotes an in-to-out swing path.
  - *Increased Power:* The closed stance can help generate additional power by encouraging a more extended backswing and a stronger release through impact.
  - *Trajectory Control:* By altering the swing path, golfers can control the ball's flight more effectively, particularly in windy conditions.
- **Applications:** The closed stance is ideal for players looking to shape their shots with a draw or to maximize power on longer shots.

MOVEMENT TECHNIQUES: WEIGHT SHIFTING AND BODY ROTATION

Effective movement within the swing is crucial in golf, allowing the golfer to maintain balance, generate power, and achieve consistent ball striking. Mastering these movement fundamentals can greatly enhance a golfer's performance on the course.

An elephant holding a golf club with a man beside it, humorously acting as a caddy

Weight Shifting

- **Purpose:** Proper weight shifting is essential for generating power and maintaining balance throughout the swing. It allows the golfer to load the back foot during the backswing and transfer weight to the front foot during the downswing.
- **Technique:**
  - *Backswing:* During the backswing, the golfer shifts weight onto the back foot, allowing for a coiled, powerful position at the top of the swing.
  - *Transition:* As the golfer begins the downswing, weight gradually shifts from the back foot to the front foot, ensuring a strong impact position.
  - *Follow-Through:* At the finish of the swing, the majority of the golfer's weight should be on the front foot, with the back foot up on its toe, indicating a complete transfer of energy.

- **Drills:** Practice weight shifting by swinging with a narrower stance to exaggerate the shift. Focus on feeling the weight move from the back foot to the front foot through impact.

Body Rotation

- **Purpose:** Body rotation is the engine of the golf swing, allowing for the generation of speed and power. Proper rotation also ensures that the club stays on the correct swing plane, leading to more accurate shots.
- **Technique:**
    - *Backswing Rotation:* As the club is taken back, the shoulders should turn around the spine, with the hips rotating slightly. The right-handed golfer's left shoulder moves under the chin, creating a powerful coil.
    - *Downswing Rotation:* The hips initiate the downswing by rotating towards the target, followed by the shoulders, arms, and hands, creating a powerful unwinding motion.
    - *Follow-Through:* Complete rotation through the ball is essential for maximizing distance and maintaining accuracy. The golfer should finish with the chest facing the target, indicating full rotation.
- **Drills:** Practice body rotation by placing a club across your shoulders and simulating the swing motion without a ball. Focus on turning the shoulders fully in the backswing and rotating the hips and shoulders through to the finish.

DRILLS TO IMPROVE STANCE AND MOVEMENT

Incorporating specific drills into training routines can significantly enhance a golfer's stance, balance, and movement capabilities. Here's an extensive guide to some of the most effective drills for mastering stance and movement in golf:

Mirror Work for Stance

- **Purpose:** Using a mirror allows golfers to visually check their stance and alignment, ensuring they adopt a consistent and balanced setup.
- **Drill:**
  - *Set Up in Front of a Mirror:* Position yourself as if addressing the ball, and use the mirror to check that your feet, hips, and shoulders are aligned with the target line.
  - *Adjust as Needed:* Make necessary adjustments to achieve a balanced, square stance. Repeat this process until it becomes second nature.
- **Benefits:** Mirror work helps reinforce proper stance and alignment, which are critical for consistent ball striking.

Swing Path Drill with Alignment Sticks

- **Purpose:** This drill helps golfers improve their swing path and body rotation, promoting a more consistent and accurate ball flight.
- **Drill:**
  - *Set Up Alignment Sticks:* Place one alignment stick on the ground along the target line and another across your toes. A third stick can be placed slightly inside the target line to guide the swing path.

- *Practice Swinging:* Focus on swinging along the correct path, using the alignment sticks as a visual guide. Ensure your body rotates naturally with the swing.
- **Benefits:** This drill helps golfers develop a repeatable swing path and improves body rotation, leading to better accuracy and power.

Balance Board Drills

- **Purpose:** Balance board drills enhance stability and weight shifting, crucial for maintaining control during the swing.
- **Drill:**
  - *Use a Balance Board:* Stand on the balance board and practice taking swings without losing balance. Focus on keeping the board level throughout the swing.

Twelve gentlemen golfers

- *Incorporate Full Swings:* As you become more comfortable, take full swings, ensuring that your weight shifts smoothly from back to front.
- **Benefits:** Balance board drills improve stability and ensure that weight shifting is controlled and consistent, leading to more powerful and accurate shots.

Mastering stance and movement is a fundamental component of success in golf. A solid stance provides the foundation for balance, control, and accuracy, while effective movement techniques enable golfers to generate power and consistency in their swings.

Types of golf clubs

5

BASIC GOLF TECHNIQUES AND COMBINATIONS: MASTERING THE FUNDAMENTALS

I N GOLF, MASTERING THE FUNDAMENTAL TECHNIQUES and strategic shot combinations is essential for developing a well-rounded game. This chapter covers the basic golf techniques—stance, grip, alignment, swing mechanics, and follow-through—as well as how to combine these elements effectively. Understanding these fundamentals will help you build a solid foundation for accuracy, consistency, and confidence on the course.

THE STANCE: THE FOUNDATION OF YOUR SWING

The stance is often referred to as the foundation of your golf swing. It provides stability, balance, and support, which are critical for accurate and powerful shots. Here's why the stance is so crucial:

Group of gentlemen and women golfers, Builth Wells Golf Club

- **Stability and Balance:** A proper stance ensures that the golfer remains balanced throughout the swing. This stability is achieved through proper weight distribution between both feet and maintaining a low center of gravity, allowing the golfer to execute a smooth and controlled swing.
- **Consistency:** A consistent stance helps golfers develop muscle memory, enabling them to replicate the same position each time they swing. This consistency is key to achieving a reliable swing and improving overall accuracy.
- **Power Generation:** The stance plays a significant role in generating power, particularly in drives and long iron shots. By positioning the feet and body correctly, golfers can maximize the energy transfer from the ground through their body and into the club.
- **Endurance:** A good stance is also about comfort and sustainability. During long rounds or practice sessions, maintaining a comfortable stance reduces fatigue and helps maintain swing quality over time.

Technique:

1. **Starting Position:** Stand with your feet shoulder-width apart, with your lead foot slightly flared out towards the target. Your weight should be evenly distributed between both feet, and your knees should be slightly flexed.
2. **Posture:** Tilt from your hips, keeping your back straight, and allow your arms to hang naturally. This posture helps in maintaining balance and creating a smooth swing path.
3. **Alignment:** Align your shoulders, hips, and feet parallel to the target line. This alignment ensures that your swing is directed towards the target.
4. **Ball Position:** The ball position varies depending on the club used. For drivers, position the ball off the inside of your lead heel. For irons, position the ball slightly back towards the center of your stance.

GRIP: CONTROLLING THE CLUB

The grip is another fundamental element of the golf swing. A proper grip ensures control over the club, affects the swing path, and directly influences accuracy. Here's how to perfect your grip:

- **Control and Stability:** A firm, consistent grip provides control over the club throughout the swing, helping to maintain the clubface's alignment for accurate shots. It also minimizes unnecessary wrist movement, which can cause the ball to veer off target.
- **Consistency:** Like the stance, a consistent grip is

essential for accurate ball striking. The grip should be firm but not too tight, allowing for a natural swing motion without tension.
- **Shot Shaping:** A proper grip can also influence the ability to shape shots, such as fades or draws, by adjusting the pressure and position of the hands on the club.

TECHNIQUE:

1. **Hand Placement:** For a neutral grip, place your lead hand on the club first, with the thumb pointing down the shaft. The V formed by your thumb and index finger should point towards your trailing shoulder.
2. **Support Hand:** Place your trailing hand on the club, with the palm facing the target. The pinky finger of the trailing hand can either interlock with or overlap the index finger of the lead hand.
3. **Thumb Position:** The trailing thumb should rest lightly on the side of the club, while the lead thumb remains securely on top.
4. **Grip Pressure:** Apply firm but even pressure with both hands. Avoid gripping too tightly, as this can cause tension and restrict the fluidity of the swing.

ALIGNMENT AND AIM: PRECISION IN EVERY SHOT

Alignment and aim are critical components of setting up for a shot. Properly aligning the body and aiming ensures that the golfer's swing path is consistent with the intended target line.

- **Alignment:** This involves positioning the feet, hips, and shoulders parallel to the target line. Proper alignment ensures that the clubface is square to the target, promoting a straight ball flight.
- **Aiming:** Aiming involves aligning the clubface with the target before setting up your stance. The clubface should be aimed directly at the target, with the body aligned parallel to the target line.

TECHNIQUE:

1. **Set the Clubface:** Before taking your stance, set the clubface behind the ball, aiming directly at the target. This ensures that the clubface is square to the target line.
2. **Align Your Body:** Position your feet, hips, and shoulders parallel to the target line. Use an alignment stick or the edge of the fairway as a reference to ensure proper alignment.
3. **Check Your Aim:** After setting up, glance down the target line to confirm that your body and clubface are correctly aligned with the target.

SWING MECHANICS: THE KEY TO POWER AND ACCURACY

Swing mechanics are arguably the most critical aspect of golf, as improper swing technique can lead to missed shots even with perfect stance and alignment.
- **Backswing:** The backswing sets the stage for the downswing and impact. A smooth, controlled backswing allows for a powerful and consistent downswing.

- **Downswing:** The downswing is where the energy generated in the backswing is transferred to the ball. Proper sequencing and timing are essential for delivering a powerful and accurate shot.
- **Follow-Through:** The follow-through completes the swing, ensuring that the energy is fully transferred to the ball and that the clubface remains square through impact.

TECHNIQUE:

1. **Backswing:** Initiate the backswing by rotating your shoulders while keeping the arms and hands in sync. The club should rise smoothly along the swing plane, with the weight shifting to the back foot.
2. **Downswing:** Start the downswing by rotating your hips towards the target while allowing the arms to follow. The hands should remain passive, allowing the clubhead to drop into the correct position for impact.
3. **Impact:** At impact, your weight should be shifted to the front foot, with the hips open to the target and the clubface square.
4. **Follow-Through:** Continue the rotation through the ball, finishing with your chest facing the target and your weight fully on the front foot.

FOLLOW-THROUGH: COMPLETING THE SWING

Follow-through is the act of maintaining the swing fundamentals (stance, grip, alignment, and swing mechanics) after the ball is struck. Proper follow-through ensures that any movements or adjustments needed are minimal, enhancing overall accuracy and power.

Golfing

- **Power Transfer:** By maintaining the swing mechanics through follow-through, golfers can ensure that all the energy generated is transferred to the ball, maximizing distance and accuracy.
- **Consistency:** Consistent follow-through helps reinforce muscle memory and makes the swing process more uniform from shot to shot.

Technique:

1. **Finish High:** After impact, allow your arms to follow the swing path naturally, finishing high with the club wrapped around your back. This indicates a full release and follow-through.
2. **Balance:** Maintain your balance through the finish, with your weight fully on the front foot. This balance is crucial for consistency and control.

3. **Hold Your Finish:** Hold your finish position until the ball lands, allowing you to assess the shot and make any necessary adjustments for the next swing.

BASIC GOLF COMBINATIONS AND THEIR USES

Combining the basic golf techniques allows players to engage the course efficiently and effectively. Here's a guide to some fundamental golf combinations and their applications:

Drive and Approach

- **Purpose:** This combination involves using a powerful drive off the tee followed by a precise approach shot to reach the green. It is essential for setting up birdie or par opportunities on longer holes.
- **Application:** Execute a controlled and powerful drive to maximize distance, followed by a well-placed approach shot to position the ball on the green. Focus on consistency in both power and accuracy.

Chip and Putt

- **Purpose:** The chip and putt combination is crucial for scoring, particularly around the greens. It involves using a short chip shot to get the ball close to the hole, followed by a putt to finish.
- **Application:** Chip the ball with a lofted club, aiming to land it softly on the green and roll towards the hole. Follow up with a confident putt to secure the score.

BASIC GOLF TECHNIQUES AND COMBINATIONS 71

Draw and Fade

- **Purpose:** The draw and fade are shot shapes used to navigate obstacles and position the ball advantageously on the fairway or green. A draw curves the ball from right to left, while a fade curves from left to right.
- **Application:** Use a draw to avoid hazards on the right and a fade to steer clear of trouble on the left. Mastering these shot shapes provides versatility and control over ball flight.

Bunker Escape

- **Purpose:** Escaping from bunkers requires specific technique and confidence. The goal is to lift the ball out of the sand and onto the green with minimal roll.
- **Application:** Open the clubface and stance, aim behind the ball, and use an aggressive, descending strike to lift the ball out of the bunker. Practice different types of bunker shots to adapt to various sand conditions.

DRILLS TO PRACTICE BASIC TECHNIQUES AND COMBINATIONS

Incorporating specific drills into your practice routine can significantly enhance your golf skills and consistency. Here are some of the most effective drills for mastering golf techniques and combinations:

Mirror Work for Alignment

- **Purpose:** Using a mirror allows golfers to visually check their alignment and setup, ensuring they adopt

a consistent and balanced stance.
- **Drill:** Set up in front of a mirror and practice aligning your body parallel to a target line. Adjust as necessary and repeat until alignment feels natural and automatic.

Impact Bag Drill

- **Purpose:** This drill focuses on improving the impact position, ensuring that the clubface is square at impact.
- **Drill:** Use an impact bag or similar object and practice striking it with your club, focusing on a solid, square impact. Repeat to reinforce proper impact mechanics.

Gate Drill for Putting

- **Purpose:** The gate drill enhances putting accuracy by helping golfers ensure the ball starts on the intended line.
- **Drill:** Place two tees slightly wider than your putter head on the green, forming a gate. Practice putting through the gate without hitting the tees, focusing on a smooth, accurate stroke.

Up and Down Drill

- **Purpose:** This drill improves short game performance, focusing on getting the ball close to the hole from various lies and then holing the putt.
- **Drill:** Drop balls in different positions around the green and practice getting up and down in two shots. Vary the distances and types of lies to simulate real-game conditions.

BASIC GOLF TECHNIQUES AND COMBINATIONS

Golfers at the Miami Biltmore Golf Club

Mastering the basic golf techniques and combinations is crucial for any aspiring golfer. The stance, grip, alignment, swing mechanics, and follow-through form the core of your golfing skills, while effective shot combinations enable you to navigate the course efficiently and strategically. Through consistent practice and targeted drills, you can enhance your technique, control, and confidence, setting the stage for success in any golfing scenario. As you develop your skills, remember that perfecting these basics is the key to becoming a more accomplished and confident golfer.

6

DEFENSIVE TECHNIQUES IN GOLF: MASTERING CONTROL AND CONSISTENCY

IN GOLF, DEFENSIVE TECHNIQUES AREN'T ABOUT warding off physical threats but rather ensuring precision, control, and adaptability in various challenging situations on the course. Effective defensive golf techniques include mastering shot control, handling difficult lies, playing from challenging positions, and developing strategic awareness. Mastering these techniques will enhance your golf skills, improve your overall game, and ensure you remain composed under pressure.

SHOT CONTROL AND TRAJECTORY MANAGEMENT

Shot control and trajectory management are fundamental defensive techniques in golf. They involve controlling the ball's flight path and ensuring consistent distance control, which is crucial for maintaining accuracy and positioning the ball effectively on the course.

DEFENSIVE TECHNIQUES IN GOLF: MASTERING

This late 13th-century manuscript margin scene is the earliest known depiction of golf, showing a game with clubs and a ball. (Bruges Public Library, Ms. 251 f. 149r)

- **Purpose:** Proper shot control helps keep the ball on target, allowing the golfer to navigate obstacles, adjust for wind conditions, and approach the green from advantageous positions. This is essential in both competitive play, where precision is key, and in casual rounds, where managing difficult courses requires skill and strategy.
- **Technique:**
    - *Grip and Stance:* Use a firm grip and balanced stance to control the club throughout the swing. Ensure your grip is consistent, with the clubface square at address, and your stance provides a stable base for the swing.
    - *Lean into the Shot:* Slightly tilt your upper body towards the target, distributing your weight towards your lead foot. This position helps control the ball's trajectory and prevents the club from digging into the turf.

- *Follow-Through:* Maintain focus on the ball and follow through after impact. Allow the club to complete its natural path, ensuring a smooth, controlled finish.
- **Drills:**
  - *Controlled Distance Drills:* Practice hitting shots with different clubs to specific targets, focusing on maintaining control and consistent distance. Start slowly and increase the difficulty by varying distances and targets.
  - *Trajectory Control Drills:* Use a lower-lofted club to practice controlling the height and spin of your shots. Focus on keeping the ball flight low in windy conditions or when playing under trees.

HANDLING DIFFICULT LIES

Handling difficult lies involves quickly diagnosing and adjusting your approach when the ball is in an unfavorable position, such as in thick rough, on a slope, or in a bunker. Mastering this skill is essential for maintaining control and preventing high scores.

- **Purpose:** Efficiently handling difficult lies prevents unnecessary strokes and ensures that you can recover effectively, even from challenging situations. This skill is critical in both competitive and recreational play, where maintaining composure under pressure is vital.
- **Technique:**
  - *Assess the Lie:* Before taking your stance, assess the lie of the ball and the surrounding conditions.

DEFENSIVE TECHNIQUES IN GOLF: MASTERING

Determine how the ball's position will affect your shot, such as its impact on club selection and swing mechanics.
- *Adjust Your Stance:* Modify your stance to accommodate the lie. For example, in thick rough, position the ball slightly back in your stance and use a steeper angle of attack to prevent the club from getting caught in the grass.
- *Controlled Swing:* Use a controlled, smooth swing to ensure solid contact. Focus on maintaining balance and adjusting your follow-through based on the lie.

- **Drills:**
  - *Difficult Lie Practice:* Set up practice sessions where you intentionally place the ball in challenging lies, such as in rough or on slopes. Practice adjusting your stance, club selection, and swing to successfully recover from these positions.
  - *Bunker Escape Drills:* Practice hitting bunker shots with different clubs and from varying distances. Focus on achieving consistent contact and controlling the ball's flight out of the sand.

PLAYING FROM UNCONVENTIONAL POSITIONS

Playing from unconventional positions is an advanced defensive technique that involves executing shots from awkward stances, such as uphill or downhill lies, or when obstructed by trees or other hazards. This skill is crucial in navigating the golf course and managing difficult holes.

Golfers at Brisbane Golf Club Tennyson 1906

- **Purpose:** Playing from unconventional positions enhances versatility and adaptability, allowing golfers to maintain accuracy and control regardless of the circumstances. This is particularly important in tournament play, where course conditions may be less than ideal.
- **Technique:**
    - *Uphill and Downhill Lies:* On uphill lies, position the ball slightly forward in your stance and align your shoulders with the slope. On downhill lies, position the ball back in your stance and swing along the slope, keeping your weight on your lead foot.
    - *Sidehill Lies:* For sidehill lies, adjust your stance to accommodate the slope. Aim to counteract the natural curve of the ball flight caused by the slope, and focus on maintaining balance throughout the swing.
    - *Obstructed Shots:* When obstructed by trees or other hazards, consider creative shot options like

a punch shot or a low fade/draw. Adjust your stance and clubface accordingly, and focus on controlled, precise swings.

- **Drills:**
  - *Lie Transition Drills:* Practice transitioning between different lies (flat to uphill, uphill to downhill) while maintaining swing control and accuracy. Focus on making necessary adjustments quickly and effectively.
  - *Obstacle Navigation Drills:* Use trees, bushes, or simulated obstacles to practice hitting around or under them. Develop a feel for controlling trajectory and shot shape in tight situations.

DEFENSIVE PUTTING TECHNIQUES

Defensive putting involves efficiently managing the green, ensuring that you can continue putting with minimal risk of three-putting. This skill is crucial in scenarios where the greens are challenging, and speed control is essential.

- **Purpose:** Proper putting techniques allow golfers to maintain momentum and avoid costly strokes on the green. Quick and smooth putting is essential for maintaining confidence and control in both competitive and casual play.
- **Technique:**
  - *Lag Putting:* When faced with long putts, focus on getting the ball close to the hole, aiming to leave an easy tap-in for the next stroke. Prioritize speed control over hole-out attempts.

- *Tactical Putting:* Conduct a tactical approach to putting when dealing with challenging greens. Assess the slope, speed, and grain before executing the stroke, and aim to minimize the chance of missing long.
- *Speed vs. Control:* Focus on both speed and control, ensuring that the putt is executed smoothly without excessive force. Proper putter handling and a consistent stroke are key.

- **Drills:**
  - Lag Putting Drills: Practice lag putting from various distances, focusing on leaving the ball within a three-foot radius of the hole. Use different green speeds to simulate tournament conditions.
  - Break Control Drills: Practice putting on greens with significant breaks, focusing on controlling the speed and direction of your putts. Track your progress by noting the consistency of your results.

MANAGING MULTIPLE CHALLENGES

Engaging multiple challenges on the course involves quickly and accurately managing different aspects of your game, such as handling wind, navigating hazards, and adjusting to changing course conditions. This skill is essential in both competitive and casual rounds, where golfers must handle various obstacles simultaneously.

- **Purpose:** Managing multiple challenges effectively enhances a golfer's ability to handle complex situations on the course, improving strategic adaptability and control.

Golf course Mikołów (Nicolei), Silesia

- **Technique:**
  - *Wind Management:* Determine the wind direction and adjust your aim and club selection accordingly. Use lower lofted clubs to reduce the impact of wind on the ball flight.
  - *Hazard Navigation:* Avoid hazards by playing smart, aiming for safer areas when necessary. If a hazard is unavoidable, plan for the best possible recovery shot.
  - *Course Management:* Use course knowledge to plan your shots strategically, considering the placement of hazards, pin positions, and green slopes.
- **Drills:**
  - *Wind Simulation Drills:* Practice hitting shots in varying wind conditions, using different clubs and shot types to maintain control. Simulate windy

conditions with fans or by practicing on exposed areas of the course.
- *Hazard Avoidance Drills:* Set up practice scenarios that require you to navigate around hazards, such as bunkers or water. Focus on precision and strategy in each shot.

Mastering defensive techniques in golf is essential for any successful golfer, whether in competitive tournaments or casual rounds. Techniques like shot control, handling difficult lies, playing from unconventional positions, defensive putting, and managing multiple challenges will significantly enhance your golf skills and overall performance. Consistent practice and application of these techniques during practice rounds will help you remain composed, adaptable, and effective, allowing you to handle any golfing scenario with confidence. As you develop your defensive skills, remember that a strong foundation in these basics is the key to excelling in golf and achieving lower scores.

Indoor golf games in Japan

The skills you develop will not only make you a better golfer but will also contribute to your growth as a disciplined, focused, and resilient individual. Whether on the course or in everyday life, the principles you learn through golf will serve you well, helping you to navigate challenges with confidence and precision.

In conclusion, defensive techniques in golf are not merely about achieving accuracy under pressure; they encompass a broader set of skills that promote safety, discipline, and personal growth. By committing to regular practice and continuously challenging yourself, you will not only excel in golf but also cultivate qualities that will benefit you in all areas of life.

7

PRACTICE GROUNDS AND PRECISION

HONING YOUR SKILLS ON THE PRACTICE RANGE: DRILLS AND TECHNIQUES FOR GOLFERS

The practice range is the crucible where every golfer forges their skills. It's more than just a place to hit balls; it's where you develop consistency, precision, and confidence. This chapter delves into what to anticipate during your range sessions, provides a variety of drills designed to refine your technique, and discusses the importance of both mental and physical preparation. By the end of this chapter, you'll understand how to maximize your time on the range and elevate your golfing prowess to new heights.

Róbert Baumgartner - Best Slovak MidAm Golf Player in 2019

PREPARING FOR PRACTICE: SETTING THE STAGE FOR SUCCESS

Understanding the Range: A Controlled Environment for Mastery

The practice range is a controlled setting where you can focus on the mechanics of your swing, experiment with different clubs, and simulate various on-course scenarios. Here's why your time at the range is crucial:

- **Real-Time Application:** Just like a live golf round, range sessions allow you to apply your knowledge and skills against real targets. The immediate feedback helps you make necessary adjustments to your swing, stance, and mental approach.
- **Simulation of On-Course Conditions:** The range offers an opportunity to practice under varying conditions—wind, different lies, and varying distances—which you may encounter on the course. This practice helps you become more adaptable and ready for whatever the course throws at you.
- **Confidence Building:** Repeated practice on the range builds muscle memory and confidence. The more you practice, the more familiar you become with your clubs and swing, translating to better performance on the course.

What to Expect on the Range

- **Structured Environment:** Your practice sessions should be well-structured, with specific goals in mind. Whether you're focusing on distance control, accuracy, or shot

shaping, approach each session with a clear purpose.
- **Engagement with Instructors:** If you're working with a golf coach, use your range time to apply the techniques and strategies discussed in lessons. Be open to feedback and corrections during these sessions.
- **Focus on Fundamentals:** Emphasize the basics during your range time—grip, stance, posture, and alignment. These fundamentals are the foundation of a consistent and reliable golf swing.
- **Respect for Etiquette and Safety:** Practice range etiquette is just as important as on-course manners. Be mindful of others around you, respect the range boundaries, and always be aware of your surroundings.

Preparation Before Hitting the Range

- **Warm-Up Routine:** Just as with any physical activity, a proper warm-up is essential before you start swinging. Light stretching, a few minutes of putting or chipping, and easy swings will get your body ready and reduce the risk of injury.
- **Equipment Check:** Ensure your golf clubs are clean and in good condition, with grips that provide a firm hold. Bring all necessary gear, including golf balls, tees, gloves, and a towel for wiping your clubs and hands.

Essential Drills for Technique and Confidence Building

Drills are the backbone of effective practice. They help isolate specific aspects of your game and allow for focused improvement.

Dry-Swing Drills: Perfecting Your Form

- **Purpose:** Dry-swing drills focus on the mechanics of your swing without the distraction of a ball. This allows you to concentrate on form, tempo, and the flow of your swing.
- **Technique:**
  - *Swing Path Focus:* Practice your swing in slow motion, paying attention to the path of the clubhead. Ensure your swing is on-plane, with the clubface square at impact.
  - *Weight Shift Drill:* Focus on the transfer of weight from your back foot to your front foot during the swing. This drill helps in generating power and maintaining balance.

Live-Ball Drills: Translating Form into Action

- **Purpose:** Live-ball drills are where theory meets practice. These drills simulate on-course situations and help in developing consistency and accuracy.
- **Technique:**
  - *Target Practice:* Set up targets at different distances and aim to hit specific areas. This drill improves accuracy and distance control.
  - *Club Selection:* Practice hitting different clubs to the same target, which helps in understanding the distance each club produces.

Movement Drills: Simulating Real Golf Situations

- **Purpose:** Movement drills mimic the actual conditions you might face on the course, such as hitting from different lies, adjusting for wind, or executing difficult shots like fades and draws.

- **Technique:**
  - *Sidehill Lie Drill:* Practice hitting from uphill and downhill lies. Focus on adjusting your stance and swing path to maintain balance and control.
  - *Bunker Shot Drill:* Work on your bunker shots by focusing on the correct entry point of the club into the sand and ensuring a smooth follow-through.

Partner Drills: Enhancing Timing and Coordination

Practicing with a partner can introduce a competitive element to your drills, pushing you to perform under pressure.

Timing and Reaction Drills

- **Purpose:** These drills are designed to improve your ability to make quick decisions and adjust your swing based on real-time feedback.
- **Technique:**
  - *Spot Drill:* Have your partner call out targets at random intervals. This drill sharpens your focus and forces you to adapt quickly to changing situations.
  - *Accuracy Challenge:* Compete with your partner to hit targets or get closest to the pin. This adds a fun, competitive edge to your practice and helps simulate match play conditions.

The Importance of Repetition and Routine

Consistency is key in golf. Regular practice, combined with structured drills and a clear focus on technique, will lead to noticeable improvements in your game.

Repetition for Muscle Memory

- **Routine Building:** Establish a pre-shot routine during practice that you can replicate on the course. This routine helps in calming nerves and maintaining focus during rounds.
- **Assessing Progress:** Keep track of your progress by noting the results of your drills and any areas for improvement. Regularly review and adjust your practice plan to address weaknesses.

Conclusion: Mastering the Art of Golf Practice

Range time is not just about hitting balls; it's about purposeful practice that builds the foundation for success on the course. By incorporating a variety of drills, focusing on the fundamentals, and maintaining a disciplined approach, you'll see steady progress in your game. Remember, the practice range is where champions are made, and your dedication here will pay dividends on the course.

Golfers Magazine March 1916 p20-21 combined

OLYMPIC SERIES: GOLF

This adapted chapter integrates the golfing content, restructured with a narrative focused on the nuances of golf practice and training. The language has been modified to fit the context of golf while maintaining a comprehensive and detailed approach.

For a powerful golf swing: set up, smooth takeaway, full shoulder turn, weight shift, solid impact, balanced follow-through

8

MENTAL MASTERY ON THE GREEN

GOLF IS A GAME THAT CHALLENGES NOT JUST YOUR physical skill but your mental fortitude as well. Success on the course demands more than a good swing; it requires a sharp mind, unwavering focus, and the ability to manage pressure with grace. This chapter delves into the mental conditioning essential for golfers, offering strategies for building concentration, resilience, and confidence, alongside techniques for visualization and managing on-course anxiety. Strengthening your mental game will elevate your performance, consistency, and enjoyment of the sport.

THE MENTAL GAME IN GOLF

Golf is as much a mental battle as it is a physical one. The ability to maintain focus, control your emotions, and stay composed under pressure often distinguishes a good golfer from a great one. Mental conditioning provides the tools you need to perform consistently and adapt to the challenges that the course throws at you.

Indoor golf in Japan

1. Importance of Mental Conditioning

- **Focus and Concentration:** Staying focused on the task at hand—whether it's a critical putt or a challenging drive—is vital. Mental conditioning hones your ability to block out distractions and maintain steady concentration throughout your round.
- **Stress Management:** The pressures of a golf round, particularly in competition, can be immense. Managing stress effectively is key to maintaining a smooth, controlled swing. Mental conditioning equips you with strategies to stay calm and composed under pressure.
- **Confidence:** Confidence in your swing, strategy, and decision-making is crucial. A confident golfer is more likely to execute shots with precision and recover quickly from mistakes. Building and sustaining confidence is a central goal of mental conditioning in golf.

2. Components of Mental Conditioning

- **Mental Toughness:** This is the ability to stay focused and resilient, especially when the game gets tough. Mental toughness helps you handle the pressure of competition, bounce back from poor shots, and maintain a positive mindset.
- **Emotional Regulation:** Golf is a game of highs and lows. Learning to manage your emotions—whether it's frustration from a missed putt or excitement after a great shot—ensures that you stay on an even keel and maintain focus.
- **Goal Setting:** Clear, realistic goals give you direction and motivation. Setting specific, achievable targets for each round or practice session helps keep you focused and provides a sense of accomplishment.

BUILDING CONFIDENCE AND RESILIENCE ON THE COURSE

Confidence and resilience are crucial for success in golf. Confidence stems from a deep belief in your abilities and preparation, while resilience enables you to recover from setbacks and maintain your focus.

1. Developing Confidence

- **Preparation and Practice:** Confidence is built through consistent, focused practice. Knowing that you've prepared thoroughly gives you the assurance to trust your swing and make decisive shots on the course.
- **Positive Self-Talk:** Replacing negative thoughts with

positive affirmations can significantly impact your performance. Remind yourself of your strengths and the effort you've put into your training.
- **Visualizing Success:** Visualization techniques reinforce confidence by allowing you to mentally rehearse successful outcomes. By imagining yourself executing perfect shots, you boost your belief in your ability to perform under pressure.

2. Building Resilience

- **Embracing Challenges:** See challenges and setbacks as opportunities for growth. Overcoming difficulties during practice and play builds resilience, making you better equipped to handle future challenges.
- **Learning from Mistakes:** Treat every mistake as a learning opportunity. Analyze what went wrong, make the necessary adjustments, and apply these lessons to improve your game.
- **Maintaining Perspective:** Keep a balanced view of your successes and failures. Understand that both are part of your development as a golfer and that each experience contributes to your overall growth.

VISUALIZATION TECHNIQUES FOR SUCCESS IN GOLF

Visualization is a powerful tool used by top athletes to enhance performance. By vividly imagining successful shots and scenarios, you can improve your focus, confidence, and overall game.

1. Understanding Visualization

- **Definition:** Visualization involves creating a detailed mental image of yourself executing successful shots. This means imagining every aspect of your performance, from the setup to the follow-through.
- **Mechanism:** Repeated visualization of successful golf scenarios train your mind to react positively and confidently in real-life situations, reinforcing the neural pathways associated with your best performances.

2. Techniques for Effective Visualization

- **Detailed Imagery:** Close your eyes and imagine every aspect of your shot—the feel of the grip, the alignment of the clubface, the swing path, and the ball's flight. Visualize each step, from setup to follow-through.
- **Positive Scenarios:** Focus on positive outcomes, such as hitting a perfect drive down the fairway or sinking a long putt. Visualization should always reinforce success, helping to build confidence and reduce performance anxiety.
- **Repetition:** Practice visualization regularly, ideally before rounds or during practice sessions. The more you visualize successful shots, the more likely you are to replicate them on the course.

MANAGING ANXIETY AND MAINTAINING FOCUS IN GOLF

Anxiety is a common challenge in golf, especially during competition. Learning to manage these feelings is essential for maintaining focus and achieving your best performance.

1. Understanding Anxiety in Golf

- **Sources:** Anxiety in golf can arise from fear of failure, pressure to perform, or the desire to meet expectations. Recognizing these sources helps in addressing them effectively.
- **Effects:** Anxiety can affect your focus, motor control, and decision-making, leading to poor shots and inconsistent performance. Managing anxiety is crucial to staying in control and playing your best.

2. Strategies for Managing Anxiety

- **Breathing Techniques:** Practice deep breathing exercises to calm your mind and body. Focusing on slow, controlled breaths can help relax your muscles and clear your mind.
    - *Example Exercise:* Inhale deeply through your nose for a count of four, hold for four counts, and exhale slowly through your mouth for a count of six. Repeat as needed to maintain calm.
- **Mindfulness and Relaxation:** Engage in mindfulness practices to stay present and focused on each shot. Techniques such as meditation or simply concentrating on your breathing can help manage anxiety and enhance concentration.
- **Pre-Round Routine:** Develop a consistent pre-round routine that includes relaxation techniques and mental preparation. A routine creates a sense of control and familiarity, helping to reduce anxiety before teeing off.
- **Positive Visualization:** Use visualization to counteract anxiety by imagining calm, controlled, and successful

performance scenarios. This shifts your focus away from fear and towards confidence.

SEEKING SUPPORT

- **Mental Coaching:** Consider working with a sports psychologist or mental coach who specializes in golf. They can help develop personalized strategies for managing anxiety, building confidence, and improving mental toughness.
- **Support Network:** Surround yourself with supportive individuals who understand the challenges of golf. Share your experiences, seek advice, and draw encouragement from coaches, teammates, and mentors.

A scene from the 'Golf Book of Hours,' circa 1540 by Simon Bening. British Library, MS 24098

THE MENTAL EDGE IN GOLF

The mental game is as vital in golf as your physical skills. By focusing on mental conditioning—developing concentration, resilience, visualization, and anxiety management—you can unlock your full potential as a golfer.

Golf stances

Square stance: The golfer's feet are aligned parallel to the target line, equidistant from the ball. This stance is optimal for precision and consistency, typically employed for standard shots where stability and control are crucial.

Closed stance: The lead foot is positioned slightly ahead of the trail foot relative to the target line. This stance favors a draw shot, generating more power and potentially greater distance, though requiring accurate control.

Open stance: The lead foot is withdrawn from the target line, promoting a fade shot. It provides greater versatility, often used to manipulate shot trajectory.

Each stance caters to specific golfing scenarios.

9

PHYSICAL CONDITIONING FOR GOLFERS

IN THE SPORT OF GOLF, PHYSICAL CONDITIONING PLAYS a pivotal role in enhancing stability, accuracy, endurance, and overall performance on the course. While golf may not demand the same levels of power or speed as other sports, it requires a comprehensive approach to conditioning that includes cardiovascular fitness, strength training, flexibility, mobility, and effective recovery. These elements combine to optimize your swing mechanics, improve consistency, and maintain mental sharpness, allowing you to perform at your best across all 18 holes. This chapter explores these aspects of physical conditioning, offering strategies to build a strong foundation for sustained success in golf.

THE IMPORTANCE OF CARDIOVASCULAR FITNESS IN GOLF

Cardiovascular fitness is crucial for golfers, as it affects stamina, focus, and the ability to maintain composure throughout a round. A well-conditioned cardiovascular system supports sustained energy levels, sharpens mental focus during long rounds, and helps maintain a steady heart rate, which is essential for executing precise shots.

Two lady golfers outside Llandrindod Wells Golf Club pavilion, one holding the Open Challenge Bowl, 1933

1. Benefits of Cardiovascular Fitness:

- **Endurance:** Cardiovascular fitness enhances your ability to maintain energy levels during an entire round of golf, which can last several hours. This endurance is critical for staying focused and making consistent swings, especially towards the end of your round.
- **Stress Management:** A strong cardiovascular system helps regulate stress and anxiety, which can impact your heart rate and stability during crucial shots. Controlling your heart rate is essential for maintaining composure and delivering a smooth swing under pressure.

- **Recovery:** Improved cardiovascular health aids in quicker recovery from the physical demands of walking the course and managing the exertion of your swing. This is particularly important when playing multiple rounds over consecutive days.

2. Cardiovascular Training Methods:

- **Steady-State Cardio:** Activities such as brisk walking, cycling, and swimming at a moderate pace improve overall cardiovascular health. Aim for 20 to 30 minutes of steady-state cardio, 3 to 4 times per week, to build a strong aerobic base that supports your endurance on the course.
- **Interval Training:** High-Intensity Interval Training (HIIT) involves alternating short bursts of intense activity with periods of lower intensity or rest. This method improves cardiovascular capacity and simulates the bursts of effort required during a round of golf, such as climbing a hill or walking between shots.
- **Golf-Specific Drills:** Incorporate drills like hill walking or timed walks over uneven terrain to mimic the physical demands of a golf course. These activities not only enhance cardiovascular fitness but also improve your stamina and endurance for the rigors of a round.

3. Incorporating Cardio into Your Training:

- **Warm-Up:** Use light cardiovascular exercises as part of your warm-up routine before practice or a round. This helps elevate your heart rate gradually, improving blood flow to your muscles and enhancing your overall performance.

- **Consistency:** Regularly include cardiovascular sessions in your weekly training plan to maintain and build endurance. Adjust the intensity and duration based on your specific goals and the demands of your golf schedule.

STRENGTH TRAINING FOR GOLFERS

Strength training is essential for improving the physical control and stability needed in golf. A well-rounded strength program focuses on enhancing the muscles involved in your swing, maintaining posture, and supporting your ability to generate power without sacrificing control.

1. Benefits of Strength Training:

- **Stability and Control:** Strength training improves your ability to maintain a consistent posture throughout your swing. Strong core and back muscles are particularly important for stability, enabling you to execute controlled and powerful swings.
- **Power Generation:** Increased strength in the upper body and legs helps generate power in your swing, contributing to greater distance off the tee and more control in your iron shots. A strong grip and forearm strength are also crucial for maintaining control throughout the swing.
- **Reduced Fatigue:** Strengthening the muscles used in your swing reduces fatigue during long rounds, helping you maintain accuracy and consistency from the first tee to the final green.

2. Key Strength Training Exercises:

- **Upper Body:**
  - *Shoulder Presses:* Use dumbbells or a barbell to perform overhead presses, strengthening the shoulders and upper back muscles crucial for a stable and powerful swing.
  - *Rows:* Bent-over rows or seated rows target the back muscles, enhancing your ability to maintain posture and control throughout your swing.
  - *Grip Strengthening:* Exercises like wrist curls, farmer's walks, and squeezing grip trainers build forearm strength, essential for a firm and consistent grip on the club.
- **Lower Body:**
  - *Squats:* Bodyweight or weighted squats build leg strength, supporting a stable base and powerful drives.
  - *Lunges:* Lunges improve leg strength and balance, aiding in the transition of weight through your swing.
- **Core:**
  - *Planks:* Planks and side planks strengthen the core muscles, providing the stability needed to maintain a consistent swing plane.
  - *Russian Twists:* This exercise targets the obliques, enhancing rotational strength and control during your swing.

3. Structuring Your Strength Training:

- **Frequency:** Incorporate strength training sessions 2 to 3 times per week, allowing adequate rest between

workouts. Balance strength training with your practice schedule to ensure comprehensive development without overtraining.
- **Progression:** Gradually increase weights and intensity to continue making progress. Focus on maintaining proper form to maximize benefits and minimize the risk of injury.
- **Integration:** Combine strength training with cardiovascular and flexibility workouts to create a balanced and effective training program that supports your overall golf performance.

FLEXIBILITY AND MOBILITY WORKOUTS FOR GOLFERS

Flexibility and mobility are essential for golfers, enabling a full range of motion, preventing injuries, and improving performance. Agility and flexibility are key to executing a smooth swing and adapting to various conditions on the course.

1. Importance of Flexibility and Mobility:

- **Range of Motion:** Enhanced flexibility allows for optimal swing mechanics, improving your ability to generate power and maintain control throughout your swing.
- **Injury Prevention:** Flexible muscles and joints reduce the risk of strains and injuries, helping you maintain peak condition throughout the season.
- **Performance Enhancement:** Improved flexibility and mobility contributes to better balance and stability,

crucial for consistent shot-making and effective recovery from challenging lies.

2. Flexibility Exercises:

- **Static Stretching:** Perform after workouts or rounds, focusing on the shoulders, back, legs, and arms.
    - *Shoulder Stretch:* Pull one arm across the chest to stretch the shoulder muscles.
    - *Hamstring Stretch:* Reach for your toes with one leg extended to stretch the hamstrings.
    - *Quadriceps Stretch:* Pull your ankle towards your glutes to stretch the quadriceps.
- **Dynamic Stretching:** Incorporate into your warm-up routine with exercises like leg swings, arm circles, and torso twists to prepare your muscles for the demands of the game.

Mrs. H. A. Jackson golfing

3. Mobility Workouts:

- **Foam Rolling:** Use foam rollers to reduce muscle tightness and enhance mobility, particularly in the lower back, hips, and shoulders.
- **Joint Mobility Drills:** Include exercises like hip circles, shoulder rotations, and ankle rolls to maintain joint flexibility and reduce stiffness.
- **Yoga:** Incorporate yoga poses such as downward dog and warrior to improve flexibility, balance, and relaxation.

4. Routine Structure:

- **Frequency:** Perform flexibility and mobility exercises 3 to 4 times per week, integrating them into your warm-up and cool-down sessions.
- **Consistency:** Gradually increase the duration and intensity of your flexibility and mobility workouts to see continuous improvement.

REST AND RECOVERY: ESSENTIAL FOR PEAK PERFORMANCE

Rest and recovery are critical components of any training program, allowing your body to repair and strengthen, reducing the risk of overtraining and injury.

1. Importance of Rest and Recovery:

- **Muscle Repair:** Rest is essential for muscle recovery and growth. Adequate rest periods allow your body to repair after intense training sessions, improving overall strength and endurance.
- **Injury Prevention:** Proper recovery helps prevent overuse injuries and reduces the risk of burnout, supporting long-term participation and success in golf.
- **Performance Optimization:** Sufficient rest improves focus, energy levels, and physical readiness, ensuring you are at your best for practice sessions and rounds.

2. Strategies for Effective Recovery:

- **Rest Days:** Incorporate at least one full rest day per week into your training schedule. Use this time to recover

fully and engage in light activities such as walking or stretching to maintain mobility.
- **Sleep:** Prioritize quality sleep to support recovery. Aim for 7 to 9 hours of sleep per night, establishing a regular sleep schedule to enhance muscle repair and overall well-being.
- **Nutrition:** A balanced diet rich in protein, carbohydrates, and healthy fats supports muscle repair and replenishes energy stores. Consider post-workout meals with adequate protein and carbs to boost recovery.
- **Hydration:** Maintain proper hydration before, during, and after training. Water supports muscle function and recovery, and staying hydrated is essential for peak physical performance.

3. Monitoring and Avoiding Overtraining:

- **Recognize Symptoms:** Be aware of overtraining symptoms such as persistent fatigue, reduced performance, and increased susceptibility to injuries. Adjust your training intensity and schedule as needed to prevent overtraining.
- **Listen to Your Body:** Pay attention to how your body feels during and after workouts. Modify your training based on your physical condition and recovery needs to avoid burnout and maximize performance.

Consult Professionals

Work with a coach or trainer to develop a balanced training plan that includes proper rest and recovery strategies. Their guidance can help tailor your program to your specific needs and goals.

OLYMPIC SERIES: GOLF

Two lady golfers with clubs, one holding a trophy

Tom Watson after winning the 1982 US Open

10

FUELING THE SWING: NUTRITION AND DIET FOR GOLFERS

THE ROLE OF NUTRITION IN GOLF

In the game of golf, where precision, focus, and endurance are key, nutrition plays a pivotal role in enhancing performance. Much like a finely tuned golf club, your body requires the right fuel to perform at its best. This chapter delves into the nuances of nutrition tailored specifically for golfers, exploring how a strategic approach to diet can improve focus, sustain energy, and aid in recovery, ensuring you're always at the top of your game.

OPTIMIZING FOCUS AND MENTAL SHARPNESS ON THE COURSE

Importance of Mental Clarity

Golf is as much a mental game as it is physical. Maintaining sharp focus and mental clarity can be the difference between a birdie and a bogey. The right nutrition supports cognitive function, allowing you to stay composed, make precise decisions, and maintain concentration through each hole.

Key Nutrients for Mental Performance:

- **Omega-3 Fatty Acids:** Found in oily fish like mackerel and salmon, as well as in flaxseeds and walnuts, omega-3s are essential for brain health. These nutrients enhance cognitive function, improve mood, and reduce stress levels—critical for maintaining calm under pressure on the golf course.
- **Antioxidants:** Foods rich in antioxidants, such as berries, dark chocolate, and green leafy vegetables, combat oxidative stress and promote brain health. This support ensures sustained mental acuity, particularly useful during long rounds and tournament play.
- **B Vitamins:** Vitamins like B6, B12, and folate are vital for brain function, energy production, and mood regulation. Sources include whole grains, eggs, and leafy greens, which contribute to overall mental sharpness and concentration.

SUSTAINING ENERGY AND ENDURANCE THROUGHOUT THE ROUND

The Importance of Stable Energy Levels

Golf requires consistent energy over several hours. Fluctuations in energy levels can lead to fatigue, loss of focus, and a decline in performance. A well-balanced diet can provide the steady energy required to maintain optimal performance from the first tee to the final putt.

Key Nutrients for Energy and Stamina:

- **Complex Carbohydrates:** Whole grains, oats, and sweet potatoes provide a slow, steady release of energy, crucial for maintaining endurance during long rounds. These foods prevent the energy crashes associated with simple sugars, ensuring you stay energized and focused.
- **Proteins:** Essential for muscle repair and endurance, proteins help maintain muscle mass and stability, crucial for a consistent swing. Include lean meats, fish, eggs, and plant-based proteins like beans and tofu in your diet.
- **Healthy Fats:** Sources like avocados, nuts, seeds, and olive oil provide long-lasting energy and are vital for overall health. These fats support a healthy nervous system, enhancing fine motor skills critical for precision shots.

MICRONUTRIENTS: ENHANCING PERFORMANCE AND RECOVERY

Supporting Overall Health

Vitamins and minerals are essential for energy production, immune function, and muscle recovery—vital for any golfer looking to perform consistently and recover quickly.

Essential Micronutrients:

- **Iron:** Vital for oxygen transport, iron-rich foods like lean meats, beans, and spinach are crucial for sustaining energy and endurance on the course.
- **Calcium and Vitamin D:** These nutrients support bone health and muscle function, important for stability and posture during play. Incorporate dairy products, leafy

greens, and fortified foods into your diet.
- **Magnesium:** Found in nuts, seeds, and whole grains, magnesium helps with muscle relaxation and prevents cramps, supporting a smooth, controlled swing.

HYDRATION: A CRUCIAL ELEMENT FOR GOLFERS

Staying Hydrated on the Course

Dehydration can significantly impair cognitive and physical performance, making proper hydration essential. Even slight dehydration can lead to reduced focus, slower reaction times, and increased fatigue.

Daily Hydration Strategies

- **Baseline Fluid Intake:** Aim to consume 2.5 to 3 liters of fluids daily, including water, herbal teas, and hydrating foods such as fruits and vegetables. Adjust intake based on climate and activity level, especially during summer rounds.
- **Signs of Dehydration:** Be mindful of symptoms like headaches, dizziness, or difficulty concentrating. A simple check is monitoring urine color; pale yellow indicates good hydration.

Adjusting Nutrition for Weight Management and Performance Balancing Weight with Performance

For golfers, particularly those competing in weight-classed events or looking to optimize performance, managing weight while maintaining energy and focus is crucial. A thoughtful approach to nutrition ensures that weight adjustments do not negatively impact your game.

Strategies for Safe Weight Management

- **Gradual Weight Changes:** Aim for a slow and steady weight adjustment, with a weekly reduction of no more than 0.5-1 kg. This method is safer and more sustainable.
- **Nutrient-Dense Foods:** Focus on foods that provide essential nutrients without excess calories. This includes lean proteins, vegetables, whole grains, and healthy fats.
- **Hydration and Weight:** Be cautious with methods involving dehydration for quick weight loss, as they can impair performance. After weighing in, rehydrate properly to restore balance.

Professional Guidance for Optimal Results

- **Consultation:** Working with a sports nutritionist can help tailor a diet plan that supports your specific needs and goals. Regular monitoring ensures the plan remains effective and safe.
- **Tracking Progress:** Keep an eye on dietary intake, weight changes, and performance metrics to ensure that your nutrition strategy is helping, not hindering, your performance.

By integrating these nutrition strategies into your routine, you'll be well-equipped to handle the physical and mental demands of golf. Proper nutrition isn't just about fueling your body; it's about giving yourself the best possible chance to perform at your peak, from the first tee to the 18th green. With the right diet, hydration, and weight management, you can enhance every aspect of your game, ensuring that you're always prepared to face the challenges of the course.

11

PRECISION MASTERY: ELEVATING YOUR GOLFING SKILLS

THE PATH TO PRECISION IN GOLF

Taking your golf game to the next level requires more than just an understanding of the fundamentals. It demands a deep dive into advanced techniques that can refine your play, enhance your control, and provide a competitive edge. This chapter explores the complexities of advanced golfing skills, including playing in challenging conditions, mastering specialized shots, perfecting your breathing techniques, honing your timing, and employing mental strategies to enhance your performance on the course.

PLAYING GOLF IN VARIED CONDITIONS

Adapting to Environmental Challenges

Golf is a sport where external elements like wind, rain, and fluctuating light conditions play a significant role in performance. Developing the ability to adapt to these environmental factors is essential for maintaining accuracy and consistency throughout your round.

Golf Costa Teguise, Sands Beach Hotel, Lanzarote

1. Playing in Windy Conditions:

- **Understanding Wind Influence:** The wind can drastically alter the trajectory of your golf ball, making it imperative to understand how wind speed and direction affect your shots.
    - *Reading the Wind:* Use visual cues such as the movement of trees, flagsticks, or ripples on water hazards to gauge wind strength and direction. Learning to read these signs will enable you to anticipate how the wind will influence your shot.
    - *Adjusting Your Shots:* Compensate for wind by altering your aim, adjusting your club choice, or modifying your swing. Practicing in various wind

conditions will help you develop the necessary feel for these adjustments.

2. Managing Light Conditions:

- **Dealing with Low Light:** Playing in low light can challenge your ability to see the ball clearly, affecting your judgment and shot execution. Understanding how to adapt to different light conditions is critical.
    - *Equipment and Techniques:* Consider using a high-visibility ball or wearing polarized sunglasses to reduce glare. Adjust your stance and focus to ensure a clear sightline to the ball.
    - *Overcoming Glare:* Glare from the sun can be distracting and impair your focus. Use a visor or cap to shield your eyes and position yourself to minimize the impact of glare on your game.

3. Managing Pressure on the Course:

- **Simulating Competitive Pressure:** The pressure of competition can affect your performance. Simulate tournament conditions during practice by introducing time constraints, competitive elements, or even an audience to build resilience.
    - *Mental Rehearsal:* Visualize yourself successfully managing pressure situations. Practice imagining your calm, confident execution of shots under challenging conditions.
    - *Controlled Breathing:* Use controlled breathing techniques to maintain focus and composure. Lowering your heart rate and reducing tension will help you stay steady during crucial moments.

UTILIZING SPECIALIZED SHOTS AND TECHNIQUES

Perfecting Your Repertoire

Advanced golfing demands mastery of a variety of shots that go beyond the basics. These specialized techniques enable you to adapt to different situations on the course, whether you're navigating hazards, making precision approaches, or dealing with challenging lies.

1. Mastering the Low Punch Shot:

- **When to Use It:** The low punch shot is ideal when you need to keep the ball under the wind or navigate around obstacles like trees.
  - *Technique:* Position the ball back in your stance and keep your hands ahead of the ball. Use a shortened backswing and focus on maintaining a low, controlled follow-through to keep the ball flight low.

2. Executing the Flop Shot:

- **High, Soft Landing:** The flop shot is essential for getting the ball to stop quickly on the green, especially when you're short-sided or need to clear a bunker.
  - *Technique:* Open your stance and clubface, and position the ball forward in your stance. Make a steep backswing, allowing the club to slide under the ball, creating a high, soft shot with minimal roll.

3. Navigating Uneven Lies:

- **Adapting to the Terrain:** Golf courses present a variety of lies, from uphill and downhill slopes to sidehill lies.

Understanding how to adjust your stance and swing to these conditions is key.

- *Uphill Lies:* For uphill lies, align your shoulders with the slope and position the ball slightly forward. Swing along the slope to maintain balance and control.
- *Downhill Lies:* For downhill lies, align your shoulders with the slope and position the ball slightly back. Use a controlled swing to maintain stability and accuracy.

MASTERING BREATHING TECHNIQUES IN GOLF

The Subtle Art of Breath Control

Breathing is an often-overlooked aspect of golf that can significantly impact your performance. Proper breathing techniques help you maintain steadiness, focus, and reduce the body's natural movements that can affect your swing.

1. The Natural Respiratory Pause:

- **Understanding the Pause:** The natural respiratory pause occurs at the end of an exhale when the body is most relaxed. This is the optimal moment to take a shot, as it minimizes body movement.
  - *Technique:* Practice timing your shots to coincide with this pause. Inhale deeply, exhale fully, and use the brief stillness to initiate your swing without rushing.

2. Controlled Breathing for High-Pressure Situations:

- **Managing Stress with Breath:** In high-pressure situations, such as competitions, controlled breathing can help maintain calm and focus. Techniques like diaphragmatic breathing are effective for managing nerves.
    - *Diaphragmatic Breathing:* Focus on deep breaths that expand your diaphragm rather than shallow chest breaths. This technique improves oxygen flow and helps maintain composure under pressure.
    - *Incorporating Breathing Drills:* Include breath control exercises in your practice routine. Start with dry swings, focusing solely on synchronizing your breath with your swing rhythm, and gradually incorporate this into live play.

STRATEGIC USE OF MENTAL VISUALIZATION IN GOLF

Harnessing the Power of the Mind

Mental visualization is a powerful tool in golf that can enhance performance by mentally preparing you for various scenarios on the course. This section explores how to effectively use mental imagery to improve focus, decision-making, and execution.

1. Visualizing Success:

- **Creating a Mental Picture:** Before each shot, take a moment to visualize the entire process, from your stance to the ball's trajectory and final resting place.

This mental rehearsal helps solidify your intention and enhances your ability to execute the shot as planned.

- *Developing Consistency:* Regularly practice mental visualization as part of your pre-shot routine. Consistency in this mental exercise will translate to greater consistency in your physical performance.

2. Overcoming Mental Barriers:

- **Breaking Through Psychological Obstacles:** Golf is as much a mental game as it is physical. Use visualization to overcome fears, doubts, and negative thoughts that may arise during play.
  - *Mental Resilience:* Train your mind to remain positive and focused, especially after a poor shot or during a challenging round. Visualize yourself recovering quickly and effectively, maintaining your composure and confidence.

Disc Golf Course warning sign at a disc golf course in Clearwater, FL

Golf exercises

12

EMBARKING ON YOUR FIRST GOLF TOURNAMENT:
A COMPREHENSIVE GUIDE

THE SIGNIFICANCE OF YOUR FIRST GOLF TOURNAMENT

Participating in your first golf tournament is not just another date on your calendar; it represents the culmination of countless hours of practice, dedication, and the pursuit of golfing excellence. It's a moment that transitions your game from practice rounds to competitive play, where your skills will be put to the test under pressure. This chapter provides a thorough exploration of the preparations needed to excel in your debut tournament, focusing on the essential blend of technical mastery, mental resilience, and meticulous logistical planning. With these aspects in check, you will approach your first tournament not just prepared but with confidence and purpose.

THE JOURNEY TO YOUR FIRST COMPETITIVE ROUND

Laying the Groundwork for Success

Your path to the first tee on tournament day involves a series of carefully planned steps, each of which is crucial for laying a solid foundation for success. From structured practice to advanced strategic planning, every phase is vital. Let's explore this journey in detail to ensure that your preparation is as comprehensive as possible.

BUILDING A STRONG FOUNDATION

Structured Practice Routine

A well-organized practice routine is the cornerstone of competitive golf. It's not just about hitting balls on the range; it's about systematically refining every aspect of your game. Begin by crafting a detailed practice plan that includes technical drills, course management, physical conditioning, and mental preparation. Divide your weekly schedule to focus on key skills such as driving accuracy, short game finesse, and putting. Each practice session should have a clear

Golf club head covers in use: Driver, Fairway Wood, Hybrid, Iron, and Putter

goal, whether it's honing your distance control, improving shot shaping, or enhancing your mental focus. Consistency and repetition are critical to developing the muscle memory needed under tournament pressure.

Technical Skill Refinement

Your proficiency in the technical aspects of golf directly impacts your tournament performance. Whether your focus is on driving, iron play, or putting, it's essential to master the fundamental elements: stance, grip, alignment, and swing tempo. Incorporate a variety of practice drills that challenge different aspects of your game, such as hitting different shot shapes, varying your club selection, and practicing under simulated pressure. Incorporating both on-course practice and range work will help solidify your techniques and expose any areas that need further refinement.

Physical Conditioning

Golf, though often seen as a game of skill, requires a considerable level of physical fitness to maintain performance throughout a round. A well-rounded conditioning routine should include:

- **Cardiovascular Training:** Engage in regular cardio exercises such as brisk walking, jogging, or cycling. These activities enhance your endurance, enabling you to maintain focus and energy levels during the latter stages of a round.
- **Strength Training:** Focus on exercises that build core stability, lower body strength, and grip endurance. Functional movements like lunges, planks, and resistance

band exercises are particularly beneficial.
- **Flexibility and Mobility:** Flexibility is crucial for maintaining a full range of motion in your swing and preventing injuries. Incorporate stretching routines, yoga, or dynamic warm-ups to keep your muscles agile and prepared for varied playing conditions.

FINDING AND ENTERING YOUR FIRST TOURNAMENT

Identifying Suitable Events

The world of competitive golf offers a wide range of tournaments catering to all skill levels. To find the right tournament, research local, regional, and national events. Golf clubs, online forums, and governing body websites are excellent resources for discovering upcoming competitions. Select events that align with your current skill level and offer a clear progression path to more advanced play. If possible, attend as a spectator before competing to familiarize yourself with the atmosphere and format.

Understanding Entry Requirements

Tournaments often have specific entry requirements, including handicap restrictions, age categories, and adherence to specific equipment standards. Thoroughly review the criteria for each event to ensure you meet all the necessary qualifications. Overlooking these details can lead to disqualification or missed opportunities, so confirm your eligibility well in advance and address any gaps.

The Registration Process

Registering for a tournament typically involves completing detailed forms, paying entry fees, and submitting proof of eligibility, such as your handicap certificate. Ensure all information is accurate before submission to avoid administrative issues. Once registered, study the tournament schedule, familiarize yourself with the course layout, and note key logistical details such as check-in times and locations. Having these details in hand will help you reduce pre-event stress and focus entirely on your performance.

PRE-TOURNAMENT PREPARATIONS

Tapering Your Practice

As the tournament approaches, it's essential to taper your practice routine to avoid fatigue while keeping your skills sharp. Focus on light drills, maintaining your routine, and visualization exercises to stay rested yet ready.

Mental Preparation

Mental readiness is just as important as physical preparation. Regularly practice visualization techniques, imagining yourself succeeding in different scenarios on the course. Incorporate relaxation methods such as deep breathing or mindfulness meditation to build resilience against competition nerves.

Equipment and Logistics

Ensure that all your equipment is in top condition well before the tournament. Inspect your clubs, balls, and any other gear you'll be using. Clean and test everything, and pack an emergency kit with spare gloves, balls, and tees to avoid any last-minute issues. Consider the logistics of your journey—whether it's a short drive or involves travel arrangements, ensure every aspect is planned to avoid last-minute complications.

WHAT TO EXPECT ON TOURNAMENT DAY

Arrival and Preparation

Early Arrival

Plan to arrive at the course early to allow ample time for check-in and to acclimatize to the environment. An early arrival also gives you the opportunity to familiarize yourself with the course, identify key locations like restrooms and practice facilities, and establish a comfortable spot to prepare your gear. Being well-settled before your tee time can significantly reduce anxiety and set a positive tone for the day.

Warm-Up Routine

Make the most of the practice facilities available. Start with some light stretching, followed by a warm-up session on the driving range and putting green. Focus on key areas of your game that will be crucial for the round ahead, such as short game touch and driving accuracy. A well-structured warm-up routine will help ease pre-tournament nerves and ensure you start your round feeling confident and prepared.

ON THE COURSE: MAINTAINING FOCUS AND COMPOSURE

Pre-Shot Routine

Establishing a consistent pre-shot routine is essential for maintaining focus and composure during your round. Whether it's a sequence of physical actions, a mental mantra, or a breathing pattern, a routine helps center your attention and calm your nerves. Stick to your routine throughout the tournament to create a sense of familiarity and control.

Managing Pressure

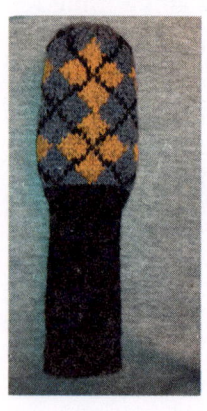

Competition brings inherent pressure, and handling it effectively is key to success. Acknowledge your nerves as a natural response to the stakes involved, and channel that energy into heightened concentration and precision. Break down each hole into manageable tasks—focus on executing each shot with deliberate intent, rather than worrying about the overall score or ranking. Keeping your mind in the present, one shot at a time, is crucial.

Argyle golf head cover

HANDLING TOURNAMENT NERVES

Recognizing Normalcy

It's important to recognize that nerves are a universal experience in competition. They signify your commitment and investment in your performance. Accepting nerves as a normal part of the process can diminish their power over you. Instead of perceiving them as a threat, view them as a sign that you care deeply about doing well.

Tiger Woods drives by Allison

Channeling Nervous Energy

Nervous energy can be redirected to enhance your performance. Use the adrenaline boost to sharpen your focus and quicken your reflexes. Stay engaged with each shot, focusing on execution rather than outcome. This shift in mindset can turn what feels like a disadvantage into a performance-enhancing state.

Relaxation Techniques

Incorporate relaxation techniques into your pre-competition routine. Methods like deep breathing, progressive muscle relaxation, or mindfulness meditation can help keep anxiety at manageable levels. Regular practice of these techniques will make them second nature, ready to be deployed when competition stress peaks.

THE ROLE OF YOUR SUPPORT TEAM

Pre-Tournament Support

In the lead-up to your tournament, your support team—be it a coach, mentor, or supportive friends and family—plays an integral role. Coaches can provide strategic advice on course management and shot selection, while your support network offers the emotional encouragement that boosts confidence. Use their insights to refine your game plan and lean on their experience to navigate any pre-tournament challenges.

On-Course Guidance

During the tournament, your support team serves as a steadying presence. They can offer quick tips between holes, help troubleshoot any equipment issues, and provide moral support to keep you grounded. Their observations from the sidelines can offer fresh perspectives and immediate feedback, helping you stay adaptable and focused throughout your round.

EMBARKING ON YOUR FIRST GOLF TOURNAMENT 131

STAND CORRECTLY   **& EXTEND YOUR LEFT ARM**

Stand correctly, extend your left arm, swing back, rotate shoulders, follow through, and repeat with the right hand

Begin in a balanced stance, smoothly take the club back, rotate fully, and follow through with a controlled finish

13

REFINING YOUR STRATEGY: ANALYZING COMPETITIONS FOR GOLF

DEVELOPING A MASTERFUL APPROACH TO GOLF COMPETITIONS

Golf is a game that demands more than just physical prowess; it requires an intricate understanding of strategy, mental fortitude, and the ability to continually refine one's approach. As golfers, our journey is defined by our capacity to learn from each round, to analyze our performance meticulously, and to make the necessary adjustments that will propel us to the next level. Whether you are vying for a title in a local club competition or setting your sights on the grandeur of professional championships, the ability to dissect your game and that of others is crucial. This chapter provides a comprehensive guide on how to scrutinize golf competitions effectively—both your performances and those of top professionals—and how to apply these insights to enhance your game continuously.

OBSERVING PROFESSIONAL GOLF COMPETITIONS: GAINING INSIGHTS FROM THE GREATS

Professional golf tournaments are an unparalleled resource for any golfer seeking to elevate their game. The precision, consistency, and strategic acumen displayed by elite golfers offer invaluable lessons that can be integrated into your own play. Watching these professionals isn't just about admiring their skills; it's about learning from their techniques, understanding their strategies, and applying these insights to your own game.

STUDYING TECHNIQUES AND DISCIPLINES

In the realm of professional golf, success hinges on the mastery of several core elements: precision, consistency, adaptability, and strategic planning. Each of these elements plays a critical role in determining the outcome of a match, and understanding how top golfers harness these elements can offer significant insights.

Precision and Consistency

Professional golfers exhibit an exceptional level of control over their shots. This control stems from a consistent form that ensures accuracy, regardless of the situation. When observing professionals, pay close attention to how they manage their stance, grip, and swing mechanics. Notice the small nuances in their posture and the fluidity of their movements—elements that contribute to their consistent performance. For instance, the way they align their body to the target, the steadiness of their hands during the swing, and their follow-through all play a crucial role in delivering precise shots. This consistency is not only a physical attribute but also a mental one, especially during high-pressure moments, such as during playoffs or when attempting a difficult putt under tournament conditions.

Golf clubs

Adaptability Across Disciplines

Golfers often participate in a variety of tournaments, each with its own set of challenges. Whether it's the unpredictability of links golf, the strategic demands of match play, or the endurance required for stroke play, adaptability is key. Professionals are adept at adjusting their approach depending on the course layout, weather conditions, and the specific demands of each hole. For example, on a links course, where the wind is a constant factor, professionals might opt for lower ball flights to control the trajectory and reduce the impact of the wind. Similarly, in match play, where the focus is on beating an opponent on each hole rather than just scoring well overall, players may take more risks to gain an advantage. Observing how professionals navigate these different scenarios can offer valuable lessons in adaptability and strategic planning.

STRATEGIC AND TACTICAL PLANNING

The ability to plan and execute a strategy effectively is what often separates the good golfers from the great ones. In professional golf, this involves meticulous planning for each shot, understanding the nuances of the course, and making strategic decisions that can influence the outcome of the game.

Course Management

One of the most critical aspects of golf is course management—how a player navigates the course with strategic precision. Professional golfers do not simply rely on their swing; they plan each shot meticulously to navigate the course effectively. This involves assessing the layout, understanding the placement of hazards, and making decisions on when to play conservatively or when to take risks. For instance, on a par-5 hole with water hazards, a professional might choose to lay up short of the hazard on their second shot, rather than going for the green, depending on their position in the tournament. This decision-making process is crucial to their success, as it involves weighing the risks and rewards of each shot and choosing the best option to maximize their chances of scoring well.

Adapting to Unforeseen Challenges

No two rounds of golf are ever the same, and professionals are adept at adapting to changing conditions. Whether it's a sudden change in weather, such as a gust of wind or a downpour, or an unexpected hazard, such as a ball landing in a divot, the ability to adapt quickly and effectively is vital. Professionals often have contingency plans in place for these situations, allowing them to adjust their strategy on the fly without losing focus. For example, if a hole plays longer due to wind, they might choose a different club or adjust their stance to account for the wind's effect on the ball. This flexibility and quick thinking are essential skills that can make the difference between a good round and a great one.

HANDLING PRESSURE IN PROFESSIONAL PLAY

Golf is as much a mental game as it is a physical one. The pressure of competition can affect even the most seasoned professionals, but those who manage it well are often the ones who come out on top.

Maintaining Composure

The mental aspect of golf cannot be overstated. Professionals are masters at keeping their cool, even when the stakes are high. This composure is achieved through a combination of mental discipline, experience, and techniques that help them stay focused and composed, especially during crucial moments, such as playoff scenarios or when making a critical putt. Observe how they manage stress during these moments—whether it's through deep breathing, positive self-talk, or visualization techniques. These strategies help them maintain their focus and execute their shots with precision, despite the pressure. Learning to manage your mental state in a similar way can greatly enhance your performance, especially in competitive settings.

REVIEWING YOUR OWN PERFORMANCE: TURNING REFLECTION INTO IMPROVEMENT

After each competition, it's essential to conduct a thorough review of your performance. This reflection should cover all aspects of your game, from your physical execution to your mental approach. By critically analyzing your own game, you can identify areas for improvement, reinforce good habits, and develop a plan for future growth.

Technical Review

The technical aspects of your game are the foundation upon which your performance is built. A detailed review of these elements is crucial for identifying strengths and weaknesses.

Shot Accuracy

Begin by analyzing the accuracy of your shots. Were you consistently hitting the fairways and greens, or did you struggle with your aim? Reviewing your scorecards and any recorded footage can help you identify patterns, such as recurring misses to one side, which may indicate issues with your swing mechanics. For example, if you notice that you consistently miss to the right, it could be a sign of an open clubface at impact or an over-the-top swing path. By identifying these patterns, you can focus your practice sessions on correcting these flaws, whether through drills, lessons, or adjustments to your equipment.

Swing Consistency

Reflect on the consistency of your swing throughout the competition. Did you maintain the same form under pressure as you did in practice? Consistency is key to performing well in golf, and any deviations in your swing can lead to mistakes. For instance, if you find that your swing becomes quicker or more aggressive under pressure, this could lead to a loss of control and accuracy. By recognizing these tendencies, you can work on maintaining a more even tempo and rhythm in your swing, regardless of the situation.

TACTICAL ANALYSIS

While the technical aspects of your game are critical, your ability to make sound tactical decisions on the course is equally important.

Execution of Strategy

Consider how well you stuck to your game plan during the competition. Did you make adjustments when necessary, or did you find yourself deviating from your strategy under pressure? Understanding where your tactical decisions succeeded or failed will help you refine your approach for future competitions. For example, if you planned to play conservatively on certain holes but found yourself taking unnecessary risks, this could indicate a lack of discipline or a need to adjust your strategy based on the conditions or your position in the tournament.

Patent golf machine (taken for Conimatti), 2 April 1938, by Sam Hood

MENTAL AND EMOTIONAL MANAGEMENT

Golf is a sport that tests not only your physical abilities but also your mental and emotional resilience. Reflecting on your mental state during the competition can provide valuable insights into how to improve your focus and composure.

Handling Competition Nerves

Reflect on your mental state during the competition. Were you able to manage your nerves, or did anxiety affect your performance? Identifying these moments can help you develop strategies to stay calm and focused in future tournaments. For example, if you find yourself getting anxious before a crucial shot, you might consider incorporating relaxation techniques, such as deep breathing or visualization, into your pre-shot routine. These techniques can help you stay calm and focused, allowing you to execute your shots with confidence.

LEARNING FROM SETBACKS: TURNING FAILURES INTO FUTURE SUCCESSES

Every golfer experiences setbacks, but the key to long-term improvement lies in how you respond to these challenges. Setbacks can be frustrating, but they also provide valuable opportunities for growth.

OBJECTIVE ANALYSIS OF SETBACKS

When analyzing setbacks, it's important to remain objective and focus on the specific aspects of your game that contributed to the outcome.

Identifying Weaknesses

Instead of focusing on the negative emotions that come with failure, use setbacks as opportunities to identify specific weaknesses in your game. Whether it's a particular type of shot, such as bunker play or putting, or a mental lapse under pressure, recognizing these areas allows you to target them in practice. For example, if you struggled with your short game during a competition, you might spend extra time on chipping and putting drills to improve your touch and feel around the greens.

Developing a Plan for Improvement

Once you've identified your weaknesses, create a targeted plan to address them. This might involve specific drills to improve your short game, lessons with a coach to refine your swing mechanics, or mental exercises to boost your concentration. For example, if you struggle with consistency in your iron play, you might work on drills that focus on improving your ball-striking and distance control. By developing a structured practice plan, you can systematically work on your weaknesses and turn them into strengths.

BUILDING RESILIENCE

Resilience is a critical component of success in golf. The ability to bounce back from a poor shot, a bad hole, or a disappointing round is what separates the great golfers from the good ones.

Learning to Bounce Back

Golf is as much about mental toughness as it is about skill. Learning to recover from a poor shot or a bad round is crucial. Develop strategies to maintain a positive mindset, even when things aren't going your way. This might involve focusing on the positives, such as the shots you hit well or the aspects of your game that have improved, rather than dwelling on the negatives. By maintaining a positive outlook, you can keep your confidence intact and approach each shot with the belief that you can succeed.

UTILIZING VIDEO AND TECHNOLOGY: LEVERAGING TOOLS FOR ENHANCED PERFORMANCE

In today's digital age, technology plays a vital role in golf training and analysis. The use of video analysis, golf apps, and statistical tracking tools can provide you with valuable insights into your game and help you make informed decisions about your training and development.

Video Analysis

One of the most effective tools for improving your golf game is video analysis. By recording your swings during practice and competitions, you can gain a deeper understanding of your technique and identify areas for improvement.

Recording Your Swing

Use video technology to record your swings during practice and competitions. Reviewing this footage can help you spot technical flaws that you might not notice in real-time. Pay attention to your posture, grip, and the fluidity of your swing. For example, you might notice that your backswing is too long or that your follow-through is incomplete. By identifying these issues, you can work on making the necessary adjustments to improve your swing mechanics.

14

THE FUTURE OF GOLF

GOLFING INTO TOMORROW: A NEW HORIZON

Golf, steeped in centuries of tradition, continues to evolve as it marches into the future. From innovative techniques and cutting-edge training methods to the profound impact of technology and the sport's growing global reach, golf is experiencing significant transformations. This chapter explores these developments, offering a comprehensive look at how golf is changing and what the future may hold for this dynamic and multifaceted sport.

EVOLVING GOLF TECHNIQUES: MASTERING THE MODERN GAME

Modern Techniques and Strategic Enhancements

- **Precision and Consistency in Play**
  - *Refining Skillsets*: Golf techniques have consistently evolved, with modern players integrating advanced skills and strategies. Today's golfers

combine traditional methods with innovative approaches to elevate their performance. This includes advancements in swing mechanics, grip optimization, and precision in shot-making, all refined through meticulous practice and analysis.
- *Advanced Training Practices*: Training methodologies have also seen significant advancements, with a greater focus on a specific skill development and strategic preparation. Golfers now employ sophisticated drills and simulation exercises to enhance their accuracy and adaptability in various golfing scenarios. These new training methods enable players to remain competitive and versatile across different types of courses and conditions.

- **The Influence of Coaching Innovations**
  - *Emerging Training Philosophies*: Coaches are increasingly adopting scientific approaches to golf training, incorporating data analysis and performance metrics into their strategies. This includes monitoring physiological responses, analyzing shot patterns, and utilizing specialized equipment to track improvements and identify areas for further development.
  - *Personalized Training Regimens*: The creation of customized training programs has become a prominent trend. Coaches now design programs that cater to individual strengths and weaknesses, optimizing training outcomes and enhancing overall performance. This personalized approach enables golfers to maximize their potential and achieve their objectives more effectively.

THE ROLE OF TECHNOLOGY IN GOLF: ENHANCING TRAINING AND PERFORMANCE

Technological Innovations: Changing the Game

- **Advanced Training Tools**
    - *Wearable Technology:* The use of wearable technology, such as smart trackers and biometric sensors, has become commonplace in golf training. These devices provide crucial data on a golfer's performance, including swing speed, muscle engagement, and shot timing. This information allows trainers and players to make informed decisions about their training regimens, ensuring optimal performance.
    - *Virtual Reality (VR) and Augmented Reality (AR):* VR and AR technologies are increasingly being utilized to simulate golf scenarios and enhance training experiences. Golfers can use VR to practice techniques, visualize complex situations, and improve their reaction times in a controlled environment. AR applications, on the other hand, can provide real-time feedback and augment training sessions with interactive elements that challenge and refine a player's skills.

Miniature copper golf equipment. Height: 55 mm. Made by Mauro Cateb, Brazilian jeweler and silversmith

- **Digital Analysis and Simulation**
    - *Enhanced Performance Evaluation*: Digital video analysis tools enable golfers and coaches to review training sessions and competition footage in detail. This technology facilitates a comprehensive breakdown of techniques, the identification of strengths and weaknesses, and the development of strategies based on empirical data. Video analysis offers a nuanced understanding of performance, allowing for targeted improvements.
    - *Simulation Software*: Simulation software is being used to create virtual golf scenarios and analyze different playing styles. This technology helps golfers prepare for various competitions and adapt their strategies accordingly. Simulations offer insights into potential outcomes and allow for precise, targeted preparation.

GLOBALIZATION OF GOLF: EXPANDING HORIZONS

The International Growth of Golf

- **Golf Around the World**
    - *Expanding the Reach*: Golf has traditionally been associated with a few countries, but it is rapidly expanding its reach across the globe. New courses are being developed in regions that were previously untapped, and more international tournaments are being introduced, broadening the sport's appeal.
    - *Emerging Markets*: Countries like China, India, and Brazil are experiencing a surge in golf's popularity,

driven by growing middle classes and increased exposure to international sporting events. This expansion is creating a new generation of golfers who bring fresh perspectives and styles to the sport.

- **Cultural Integration**
  - *Adaptation of Local Cultures*: As golf spreads to new regions, it is also integrating aspects of local cultures. This includes the design of golf courses that reflect the natural landscapes and cultural heritage of the region, as well as the incorporation of local customs and traditions into the sport.
  - *Diversity in Participation*: The globalization of golf is leading to greater diversity among its participants. Golf is becoming more inclusive, with increased participation from women, young people, and players from diverse ethnic and cultural backgrounds. This diversity enriches the sport, bringing in new ideas and perspectives.

THE FUTURE OF GOLF COMPETITIONS: ELEVATING THE GAME

Evolution of Competitive Golf

- **Modern Tournament Structures**
  - *Innovation in Formats*: Golf tournaments are evolving to include more dynamic and spectator-friendly formats. This includes the introduction of shorter, more intense competitions, as well as mixed-gender and team events that add a new dimension to traditional play.

- *Sustainability Initiatives*: Many tournaments also focus on sustainability, incorporating eco-friendly practices into the organization and management of events. This includes the use of renewable energy, waste reduction strategies, and the promotion of environmental awareness among participants and spectators.
- **Enhancing Viewer Engagement**
  - *Interactive Broadcasting*: Advances in broadcasting technology are making golf more accessible and engaging for viewers. Interactive features, such as real-time stats, player insights, and multi-angle views, are enhancing the viewing experience and attracting a wider audience.
  - *Virtual and Augmented Reality*: VR and AR are also being used to bring viewers closer to the action, allowing them to experience the game from the perspective of the players. These technologies are revolutionizing how fans interact with the sport, making it more immersive and exciting.

EMBRACING THE FUTURE: THE ROAD AHEAD FOR GOLF

Golf's Path Forward

- **Sustainability in Golf**
  - *Environmental Responsibility*: As the world becomes more environmentally conscious, the golf industry is taking steps to reduce its ecological footprint. This includes the development of sustainable courses, the

use of eco-friendly materials in equipment, and the implementation of conservation practices to protect natural resources.
  - *Community Engagement*: Golf is also playing a role in promoting social responsibility. Initiatives such as community outreach programs, youth development projects, and charity events are helping to make the sport more inclusive and socially beneficial.
- **Technological Advancements**
  - *The Role of AI and Machine Learning*: The future of golf will likely see an increased use of artificial intelligence and machine learning in training and performance analysis. These technologies will enable more precise and personalized coaching, helping players to optimize their game in ways that were previously unimaginable.
  - *Smart Equipment*: The development of smart golf equipment, such as clubs with built-in sensors and balls with tracking capabilities, will further revolutionize the sport. These innovations will provide players with real-time data on their performance, allowing for immediate adjustments and improvements.

15

NURTURING THE NEXT OLYMPIC GOLFER

TEEING UP THE FUTURE

Raising a future Olympic golfer requires patience, structure, and well-rounded support. Golf is a sport that demands a unique combination of mental resilience, physical control, and technical mastery. Parents and coaches play a vital role in helping young athletes navigate the demanding path to the highest levels of the sport. Although the road to the Olympics may be long, it is filled with opportunities for growth, skill development, and success. Here's how to best support your child's journey toward becoming a top-level golfer.

1. Starting from the Tee: Building the Basics

Introducing your child to golf at a young age, typically between 5 and 7 years old, helps lay the groundwork for developing essential skills like hand-eye coordination, balance, and patience. During this early phase, the focus should be placed on enjoyment and having fun with the game rather than competition. Activities like mini-golf or simple driving range sessions can spark interest without overwhelming them.

Choosing a golf club or facility that has certified instructors who specialize in youth development is crucial. These professionals should create a nurturing environment where the focus is on safety, skill-building, and fostering a love for the game.

2. Driving Passion Without Overloading the Bag

While golf should be a key focus, allowing your child to engage in other sports like swimming or tennis will help in their overall athletic development. Cross-training can improve flexibility and balance, two crucial components in a successful golf swing. More importantly, it keeps the experience fresh and fun, helping to avoid burnout.

Encourage the small victories, whether it's sinking their first putt or hitting a solid drive. Instead of stressing tournament results, celebrate improvements in technique and personal progress. This approach helps build resilience and a positive relationship with the game.

3. Hitting the Fairway: Structured Coaching and Training

As your child progresses, structured training becomes essential. Early practice might start with a few sessions per week, but as your young golfer grows, they may need to practice daily or engage in more frequent training sessions. By their teenage years, serious golfers may spend up to 20 hours a week honing their skills.

Expert coaching is vital at this stage. Seek out instructors with competitive experience who understand the mental and physical demands of golf. These coaches should provide a balanced training program that includes technical skill development, mental conditioning, and course management strategies.

4. Fueling the Swing: Nutrition and Recovery

Proper nutrition is critical for supporting the physical and mental demands of golf. A balanced diet of lean proteins, complex carbohydrates, and healthy fats will help your child maintain energy and focus during long practice sessions or rounds. Hydration is also key, especially during tournaments or long practice days.

Recovery is just as important as training. Ensure that your child gets adequate sleep and takes rest days, particularly after intense practice sessions. Practices such as stretching, light yoga, or massage can help alleviate muscle soreness and improve flexibility, which is vital for maintaining an effective golf swing.

5. Avoiding Hazards: Injury Prevention and Technique

Injury prevention in golf revolves around proper technique and pacing. A good coach will emphasize correct posture, grip, and swing mechanics to reduce strain on the body, especially in the back, shoulders, and wrists. Overuse injuries can be common in young golfers, so it's important to incorporate rest and recovery into their training routine.

If an injury does occur, address it promptly by consulting

a sports medicine specialist. Rushing back into play without proper recovery can lead to long-term damage. A structured rehabilitation plan ensures a safe return to the course.

6. Balancing the Round: Managing Golf and Life

As your child becomes more involved in competitive golf, managing the balance between school, social life, and sport becomes essential. Effective time management helps to prevent burnout and ensures that golf does not overshadow other important aspects of one's life. Encouraging friendships and hobbies outside of golf will help your child develop a well-rounded and enjoyable life.

Remember, the journey to the Olympics is more like a marathon than a sprint. Celebrate your child's passion and commitment, not just their wins. A positive and supportive environment will help them remain motivated and excited about golf, regardless of tournament outcomes.

Raising a future Olympic golfer requires a careful blend of early engagement, structured training, and unwavering support. By fostering a passion for the sport while maintaining balance, you can guide your child toward success—whether that means reaching the Olympic stage or simply cultivating a lifelong love for the game. With the right guidance and dedication, the fairway to the future will be a rewarding one.

16

FILIPINO OLYMPIANS IN GOLF SPORTS

GOLF IN THE PHILIPPINES HAS A DEEP-ROOTED history. The country's golfing journey has been shaped by notable athletes, historic tournaments, and international recognition, with its pinnacle moments being performances on prestigious stages like the Olympic Games. Golfers like Yuka Saso, Bianca Pagdanganan, and Dottie Ardina have carried Philippine pride into the global spotlight, competing at the highest levels and inspiring future generations.

The introduction of golf to the Philippines dates back to 1886, when British employees working for the Manila Railway Company set up the first golf course in the paddy fields south of Intramuros, Manila. These early courses were rudimentary, but they set the stage for what would become a thriving sport in the country. By 1901, during the American colonial period, a more formal nine-hole golf course was established, leading to the creation of the Manila Golf Club. It was here that the seeds of professional and competitive golf in the Philippines were planted.

One of the most significant moments in Philippine golf came in 1913 with the founding of the Philippine Open, the oldest national golf championship in Asia. For years, Filipinos were not initially allowed to compete. However, that changed in 1929 when Larry Montes, a former caddy, became the first Filipino to win the Philippine Open, breaking barriers and setting a precedent for local players to excel on the international stage.

The Philippine Open tournament is primarily held at the Wack Wack Golf & Country Club, a venue known for its inclusivity, which allowed players of all races to participate. Founded by William "Bill" Shaw, this club became a beacon for Filipino golfers, allows them to hone their skills and compete alongside international players.

The tournament attracted notable golfers such as Sam Snead, Gary Player, and Seve Ballesteros, who played at Asian Tour events held in Manila. The Philippines became a favored destination for international competitions, further cementing its status in the golfing world. Filipino golfers like Ben Arda, Rudy Labares, and Frankie Miñoza competed at a high level, with Miñoza going on to make waves in the Asian Professional Tour.

In the modern era, the Philippines has continued to produce top-tier golfers. Yuka Saso, a Filipino-Japanese golfer, made history by winning the U.S. Women's Open in 2021, becoming the first Filipino to win a major championship. After winning gold medals at the 2018 Asian Games in both the individual and team events, Saso turned professional and began competing on the LPGA Tour. In 2024, she achieved another historic feat by securing her second U.S. Women's Open title, solidifying her status as one of the sport's elites.

Yuka Saso 2022 stamp of the Philippines

Golf made its return to the Olympic Games in 2016 after a 112-year absence, providing Filipino golfers with a new platform to showcase their talents. In the 2024

Paris Olympics, Bianca Pagdanganan and Dottie Ardina represented the Philippines in the women's golf event.

Pagdanganan's performance was particularly notable as she finished just outside of medal contention, tying for fourth place—an achievement that stands as the highest Olympic golf finish by a Filipino athlete. The course at Le Golf National in Saint-Quentin-en-Yvelines, France, posed numerous challenges, but Pagdanganan demonstrated exceptional skill and resilience, finishing with a final-round score of 68. Her near-podium finish was a proud moment for the Philippines, especially considering the highly competitive field, which included past major champions and former world number one.

Philippine President Ferdinand E. Marcos playing golf

The future of golf in the Philippines looks promising. The success of golfers like Saso, Pagdanganan, and Ardina at international competitions, including the Olympics, has inspired a new generation of athletes. With the continued support of the National Golf Association of the Philippines (NGAP) and other governing bodies, the country is poised to become a more formidable force in the sport.

In recent years, the Philippines has hosted numerous international golf events, such as the Resorts World Manila Masters.

LIST OF OLYMPIC MEDALISTS IN GOLF (1900, 1904, 2016-2024)

MEN'S INDIVIDUAL

Games	Gold	Silver	Bronze
1900 Paris details	Charles Sands 🇺🇸 United States	Walter Rutherford 🇬🇧 Great Britain	David Robertson 🇬🇧 Great Britain
1904 St. Louis details	George Lyon 🇨🇦 Canada	Chandler Egan 🇺🇸 United States	Burt McKinnie 🇺🇸 United States Francis Newton 🇺🇸 United States
1906–2012	*not included in the Olympic program*		
2016 Rio de Janeiro details	Justin Rose 🇬🇧 Great Britain	Henrik Stenson 🇸🇪 Sweden	Matt Kuchar 🇺🇸 United States
2020 Tokyo details	Xander Schauffele 🇺🇸 United States	Rory Sabbatini 🇸🇰 Slovakia	Pan Cheng-tsung 🇹🇼 Chinese Taipei

| 2024 Paris details | Scottie Scheffler United States | Tommy Fleetwood Great Britain | Hideki Matsuyama Japan |

Women's individual
(1900, 2016-2024)

Games	Gold	Silver	Bronze
1900 Paris details	Margaret Abbott United States	Pauline Whittier United States	Daria Pratt United States
1904–2012	*not included in the Olympic program*		
2016 Rio de Janeiro details	Inbee Park South Korea	Lydia Ko New Zealand	Shanshan Feng China
2020 Tokyo details	Nelly Korda United States	Mone Inami Japan	Lydia Ko New Zealand
2024 Paris details	Lydia Ko New Zealand	Esther Henseleit Germany	Lin Xiyu China